The Crisis
and the
KINGDOM

The Crisis
and the
KINGDOM

Economics, Scripture, and
the Global Financial Crisis

E. PHILIP DAVIS

 CASCADE *Books* · Eugene, Oregon

THE CRISIS AND THE KINGDOM
Economics, Scripture, and the Global Financial Crisis

Cascade Books
An Imprint of Wipf and Stock Publishers
199 W. 8th Ave., Suite 3
Eugene, OR 97401

www.wipfandstock.com

ISBN 13: 978-1-61097-476-9

Cataloging-in-Publication data:

Davis, E. P. (E. Philip), 1957–

The crisis and the kingdom : economics, Scripture, and the global financial
crisis / E. Philip Davis.

xxx + 130 p. ; 23 cm. Includes bibliographical references and index.

ISBN 13: 978-1-61097-476-9

1. Global Financial Crisis, 2008–2009. 2. Economics—Religious aspects—
Christianity. 3. Economics in the Bible. 4. Capitalism. 5. Financial crises. 6. Debt.
I. Title.

BS670 D14 2012

Manufactured in the U.S.A.

Dedicated to the memory of

Rev. Martin Levey, scientist, missionary, and pastor.

*"Your kingdom come, your will be done
on earth as it is in heaven."*

Matthew 6:10

Contents

Foreword

The economic crisis that began in 2007 had, and continues to have, a profound impact on individuals and families, churches and charities, institutions and governments. Yet when it broke, most church leaders were ill equipped to say anything helpful about it. Given the apparent complexity of the issues, which had seemingly caught even most of the experts unawares, perhaps we should be sympathetic to their bewilderment. Where people did not choose the path of silence, they often resorted to the knee-jerk reaction of denouncing the greed of bankers and consequently generated more heat than light.

Now Philip Davis' book comes to our aid and shows us "a more excellent way." No one is better suited to write this book. As an established academic economist and financial expert, who is now pastor of an inner-city London church, he proves to be a sure guide. There are at least two impressive features about this book that are characteristic of the Philip I have come to know and appreciate since he, eminent economics professor though he already was, enrolled as an undergraduate student at London School of Theology.

First, Philip writes with an enviable clarity, carefully and lucidly explaining complex economic phenomena. Readers need have no fear that they will not be able to understand the explanation of what went wrong when the global economic tsunami hit our lives. Even if the book achieved nothing else (and it achieves plenty more!), it would be valuable as an introduction to the way the capitalist economic system works. Immense learning does not always enable an author to write in a way layfolk can understand. But it does in this case.

Starting with the basic principles underlying the contemporary approach to economics, Philip then walks us through the way these work out in the financial sector, how they affect our household budgets, and the role of the government. In each area Philip provides a helpful and measured, yet concise, critique and refuses to go for the attention-grabbing headline approach of the popular press (or the popular preacher!). He does *not* believe we should overthrow capitalism as "banks and modern financial markets are essential to the modern economy" but he *does* believe they could be made to work better and that their excesses can be curbed. That leads us to the second major concern of the book, and its second major contribution.

Philip critiques each part of the economic system from a biblical viewpoint. Economics builds on a limited view of humanity. Theology offers "a more rounded and complete" view of human beings. To give this more rounded view, Philip turns especially to the teaching of the Wisdom literature in Scripture, but his biblical critique also considers the early chapters of Genesis, the teaching of Jesus, and much else besides.

Again, Philip's writing is based on a solid scholarly foundation. He knows it is foolish to pretend that Scripture neatly addresses our sophisticated modern financial system, but there are in the Bible plenty of underlying ethical issues and much wisdom about business practices and personal finances that are relevant. His admirable clarity doesn't desert him in these chapters, and I can hear his black-majority congregation in London responding enthusiastically were he to preach some of this to them.

In all this Philip provides us with the model of how to speak to contemporary issues as Christians. Here is a valuable example of how to handle the word of God in a way that intelligently releases it from its ancient culture and applies it prudently to our own day. I recall a comment David Jenkins, erstwhile Bishop of Durham, once made about Anglican bishops. He complained, "Generally speaking, bishops are generally speaking." Philip's writing will show us how to avoid falling into that trap without falling into the opposite trap of becoming dogmatic party politicians.

While the book may be easily read, it will also repay careful study and reflection. It is a prophetic book in the style of Haggai, who, many

centuries ago during another time of economic crisis, invited his au-
dience to "give careful thought to your ways." Hopefully *The Crisis and
the Kingdom* will encourage us to do just that.

DEREK TIDBALL
Former Principal of London School of Theology

Preface

This book is the culmination of a personal journey of realization of the limitations of the worldview of economics, with which I have worked for all my adult life and which dominates many aspects of modern life. Certainly at university we were taught that there are some "mavericks" who think that issues of community and altruism should be part of an economist's worldview. But apart from that we were taught uniformly that the best way to summarize human action —and even ethics—is to assume people seek to maximize their personal benefit in the pursuit of self-interest.

Becoming a Christian, as I did in 1997, brought in a different set of values but I now realize that for a number of years afterwards I was operating in two mental compartments, one "spiritual," in my church and family activities, and another "secular," in my ongoing career as a professional economist. It was when studying theology as a mature student in the mid-2000s at London School of Theology that I really began to get to grips with the limitations of economics as a way of interpreting the world and as a guide to ethical practice. In my dissertation on poverty in Africa,[1] I saw clearly that economic analyses rely on an excessively narrow view of human motivation, which may vitiate secular attempts to aid development. A blend of biblical understanding and economic insight is needed for a genuine transformation of the lives of the poor to take place.

It was against this background, and my call into church ministry, that I attended a UK Evangelical Alliance meeting on February 5, 2009. The meeting covered the issue of personal debt in the UK under the

1. See Davis (2007).

heading "Is There Life Beyond Debt?" There were a variety of speakers but none took a Christian-economics standpoint. Against the background of my expertise but also my developing understanding of economics' limitations, I saw a gap there and so did the Evangelical Alliance. They asked at the end of the meeting whether anyone was willing to help in their forward thinking, notably in the areas of theological understanding of economics and finance and their application to the ongoing financial crisis. This I was willing to do, and so I undertook the initial thinking that culminated in this book.

To me the core lesson is that over the 2000s, a variety of actors in the economy—the banks, many households, and the government—acted to maximize their personal benefit in the pursuit of self-interest. This is precisely as economic theory predicts. Bankers were seeking higher remuneration, households more consumption, and governments to be popular. But there were flaws in the rationality of each of their approaches, with adverse consequences ensuing. Some bankers lost their jobs, many households became mired in debt, and government finances are out of control in many countries. Irrationality is contrary to the expectations of economic theory but strongly in line with the biblical view of the fall of humanity and humankind's imperfection and weakness. Underlying this, we see common aspects of the greed, selfishness, and impatience of many individuals in all three aspects of the crisis.

In outlining a biblical approach to the financial crisis in confrontation with that of economics, I am, in effect, undertaking a critique of the overall aims of individuals as assumed by economics—wealth, consumption, power—in contrast to Jesus' proclamation of the kingdom of God, the law of love for God and neighbor, and responsible stewardship of resources. I strongly believe that it is the duty of Christians to better understand economics, arguably the "ruling paradigm" in today's society and government. The theologian Jürgen Moltmann was, in my view, spot-on in saying, "The neglect of economics is a wound in the side of the church."[2] And the financial crisis brings this point home particularly strongly.

Against this background, my prayer is that this book will equip Christians to better understand the crisis, to furnish the church with

2. Quoted in Dickinson and Langley (2009), 21.

a distinctive voice in these troubled times, and to press for radical Christian solutions to address the underlying difficulties. With the aims of "rational economic humanity" having been taken largely on board by policymakers, there is a vital need for the church to energetically broadcast and urge the benefits of the alternative kingdom approach.

E. PHILIP DAVIS
Penge Baptist Church
National Institute of Economic and Social Research
www.ephilipdavis.com
www.pengebaptist.org

rational behavior ≠
Responsible behavior

Acknowledgments

I would like to thank Derek Tidball for his encouragement and for preparing the foreword, and also Philip Booth, Don Horrocks, Paul Mills, and members of the UK Evangelical Alliance Advisory Group (Paul Bickley, Malcolm Brown, Niall Cooper, James Featherby, Andy Flannagan, Andy Hartrop, John Hayward, Richard Higginson, Grant Masom, Paul Morrison, Ann Pettifor, Jonathan Thornton, and Keith Tondeur) for helpful suggestions. I thank Steve Holmes and David McIlroy for detailed comments on an earlier draft as well as Daniel Webster for assistance with preparation of the Executive Summary.

Introduction

The financial crisis that began in 2007 is widely seen as the most serious and far-reaching economic event since the Great Depression of the 1930s. And yet the volume of analysis from a *Christian*, as opposed to an economic or financial, perspective has been relatively small to date.[3] There is a risk that Christians will lack a critical voice in current debates, and hence the voice of the church will be seen as irrelevant. This would be a travesty because, in fact, the Bible has a great deal of distinctive analysis to contribute, especially when set alongside the ruling paradigm of today, that of economics.

In this context, this book has three aims. First, it seeks to provide distinctive Christian-economics analyses of the crisis and its aftermath, deriving policy implications from a biblical point of view, informed by economic thought—giving the church a distinctive voice in a time of economic crisis. Second, it aims to provide material for Christians and others seeking to understand and interpret the crisis. And third, it seeks to highlight in a prophetic manner Christian solutions to some of the current difficulties. The book focuses on three key aspects of the crisis, which are common to most of the countries involved: (a) understanding the role and incentives of the bankers, (b) the plight of households with indebtedness, and (c) the massive rise in public debt.

The book is founded on the approach of the Wisdom literature of the Bible. Accordingly, it seeks to undertake a dialogue with secular forms of understanding, such as economics, while also offering a critique from the point of view of the fundamental truth of the gospel, a point developed in more detail in chapter 2. Furthermore, the main

3. Exceptions include Booth (2010) and Mills (2011).

approach in this book is to draw insights from specific biblical texts. These should not, however, be seen as separate from the broader approach of biblical teaching. Accordingly, these points are complemented, where appropriate, by some broader witness from the theological tradition. This helps demonstrate that the biblical interpretations offered are not idiosyncratic but have a deep connection to centuries of Christian reflection on the Scriptures.

The text is structured as follows; after a brief summary section giving an overview of the argument, in the first chapter we outline the events of the financial crisis from a descriptive stance, albeit informed by financial economics. This is complemented by a second chapter that contrasts the views of humanity offered by economics and by biblical theology. With these as background, we proceed to three main chapters on the role of bank employees, household debt, and public debt. In each case we present considerations from economic theory and then offer some theological reflections, following which we seek to identify tensions and complementarities between them, aiming to arrive, in turn, at policy or other prescriptive suggestions, titled "ways forward." In the final chapter, we seek to bring together these suggestions and sketch a proposed overall Christian response to recent events.

All in all, the book suggests that following the way of God's kingdom in relevant aspects of finance would have limited the amplitude of the current crisis and can help prevent future ones—while economics, by contrast, shows its limitations both as an explanation of the past and as a guide to the future. And this is as should be expected—the Bible, as God's "maker's manual" for human life, focuses on *all* of his creation, with our work lives and economic issues being as central as the spiritual.[4] The Bible utterly rejects, as this book does, the idea of a secular/sacred divide where the duty of Christians is only to focus on private faith and church-related ministry rather than on matters linked to their work lives, public policy, and economic concerns.[5]

---

4. Indeed, there are 500 Bible passages on prayer, 500 on faith but 2,350 on money.

5. On the sacred/secular divide and the damage it inflicts on the effectiveness of the church, see Greene (2010).

Summary

I write from a background as a professional economist, whose research has focused on financial instability, but who as a pastor and theologian is also interested in the interface between economics, finance, and God's kingdom. Accordingly, this book aims to provide a distinctive Christian-economics analysis of the financial crisis and proposes, in a prophetic manner, some radical solutions to the current difficulties. It focuses on the roles and incentives of bankers, the plight of indebted households, and the massive rise in public debt. Particular reference is made to experience of the US and the UK, although many of the aspects identified are relevant more widely. This summary provides a brief overview of the book, chapter by chapter.

CHAPTER 1: EVENTS OF THE CRISIS

The crisis was preceded by a credit boom, financial innovations, risk taking, and an asset price bubble in many countries, but notably the US, UK, Ireland, Iceland, and Spain. These were common features of past crises, making it surprising that this one was not better forecast. The crisis originated in the US sub-prime mortgage lending market but the size and global integration of the US financial markets made it inevitable that the crisis would become global. Housing booms and massive household debt burdens in countries such as the UK, Ireland, Iceland, and Spain, as well as the size of their financial sectors, made their economies highly vulnerable to the crisis.

CHAPTER 2: COMPARING THE VIEW OF HUMANKIND FROM ECONOMICS AND THEOLOGY

Christians need to take a step back from the crisis to understand it fully, engaging not only with biblical theology but also with economics. As in the book of Proverbs, Christians need to learn from fields of secular knowledge such as economics, while engaging in a critical dialogue that challenges such secular wisdom from the viewpoint of the truth of the gospel.

2.1 Economics—Today's Ruling Paradigm

As a social science, economics understands human actions in terms of *motives* and not simply in terms of cause and effect. Economics is inevitably "normative" (i.e., it asks how things *should* be) as well as "positive" (examining how things *are*). This is because values cannot be readily separated from facts when human nature is the subject matter.

For mainstream "positive" economics, human motivation is based on self-interest. Accordingly, there is no intrinsic value to community life, relationships, or ethical goals like poverty relief. "Normative" economics typically asserts that given a distribution of assets in the economy, the pursuit of self-interest will lead to an optimal outcome for all. Taken to its extreme, such an approach leads to laissez-faire policies and tends to exclude considerations of justice.

Economics and its view of humanity offer a good diagnostic analysis of policy issues and economic development. Yet it is weak normatively due to its focus on efficiency rather than values. Whereas virtues such as trustworthiness and honesty are vital for the smooth running of the economy, irresponsibility and immoral behavior can only be condemned in the economics framework if they are "irrationally" contrary to the self-interest of the individual perpetrator.

2.2 A Biblical View of Humankind

Like economics, theology looks both at how things *are* and how they *ought to be*. Humanity, although made in the image of God, is fallen. Therefore, choices and actions are indeed often determined by self-interest, relationships can be spoiled by power and fear, humanity may exploit nature, and work can become toil.

A biblical view of humanity is more rounded than that of economics, for it perceives that community life—not just individual fulfillment—is crucial. While at times wealth is celebrated as indicating God's blessing, it is the relationship with God that a Christian sees as central to well-being.

Being made in the image of God, we have free choice but also responsibility. Our choices may lead to money becoming an idol and the economic system becoming pervaded by "structural injustices," which disadvantages those with the least resources. Indeed, the strong normative element of the Bible has *justice at the core*. Accordingly, we contend that taking a stand on economic issues is a Christian duty, with underlying concerns focused on aspects such as stewardship, useful work, protection for the vulnerable, and preservation of family life. Equally, whereas the state is ordained by God to keep the peace and administer justice, its decisions should still be monitored critically.

Economics and the market-based economy have provided considerable benefits to society, but from a Christian point of view there remains unease with the lack of moral foundations of economics, including its narrow view of what it is to be human. We see these tensions illustrated as we examine, in turn, the incentives of bankers, the plight of indebted households, and the massive rise in public debt both from an economics and a theological point of view.

CHAPTER 3: THE FINANCIAL SECTOR—INCENTIVES TO UNDERESTIMATE RISKS

3.1 Economic Perspective

Widespread bank failures are extremely damaging to the economy, risking, as they do, a breakdown of credit provision or even the mechanism for making day-to-day payments. This helps explain both the amplitude of the recent downturn and the efforts by governments to support banks.

The performance of banking functions requires integrity and prudence on the part of bankers—virtues evidently lacking in many institutions in recent years. Underlying this lack of integrity and prudence was a combination of the bonus culture of banks and the "safety net" provided by the government. The background to strategic decisions taken by many banks was that they—and those who funded them—judged themselves to be "too big to fail." The resulting "moral hazard" gave an incentive to underprice risk and perhaps also obscured the risks they were taking.

Lack of insight was also a part of the problem. People believed that "this time was different" and forgot lessons of the past, namely that a credit and asset price boom often ends in a financial crisis.

Economics suggests that people such as bankers will act in a trustworthy manner in an ongoing relationship, such as with their employers or clients, so as to keep the benefits of that relationship. But the relationship will be abandoned if it ceases to be beneficial. The form of banking that developed in many countries in the 2000s devalued relationships generally, both within institutions and between borrowers and lenders. This, in turn, made financial relations in general, and lending in particular, more impersonal and hence vulnerable to self-interested choices.

While economics offers an understanding of banks and the incentives and motivations for bankers' behavior, it is silent on the issues of prudence, trust, and honesty that are essential to the functioning of the financial markets in the long term.

3.2 Theological Perspective

Scripture directly addresses ethical issues relevant to modern finance. The fall of Adam and Eve in Genesis 3, for example, entailed *corruption in human relationships*. Such corruption was seen recently where traders competed with one another to maximize their bonuses. And, in the same way as Adam and Eve, bankers sought *to avoid responsibility* for adverse outcomes for the firm as a whole. ↳ everyone did too

The biblical picture of human character and motivation shows realism about our frequent irrationality that seems missing from much economic analysis. The Bible is replete with examples of such behavior, including the Israelites worshipping handcrafted gods. The Bible also highlights kingdom virtues such as honesty, putting others' interests before one's own, and due diligence that were absent in many firms during the banking crisis.

Jesus seemed to accept, as a given reality, the trade of finance, but was opposed to the intrusion of commercialism in relationships with

God, and thus he drove the money changers out of the temple. Paul warns that "people who want to get rich fall into temptation and a trap," and many bankers did just that—falling into the temptation to cut corners in prudence, diligence, and risk assessment, and in some cases ruining themselves and their firms as a consequence.

Jesus once said: "you cannot serve both God and money." The implication is that we cannot serve God if our attitude to money is to see it as a *goal* in life, an end in itself, ultimately an idol. Wealth can entice us into pride, selfishness, and greed, while up to 2007 society came falsely to value financial sector employment above other forms of work.

3.3 Ways Forward

Theology questions whether banking regulation, aimed to maintain financial stability, can ever be sufficient. Even promoting *values* among bankers may end up with pious lists to write on the wall, which are then ignored or circumvented. Crucially, these should be complemented by *virtues* such as honesty, prudence, courage, and justice, the internal conviction of what is right behavior, and the determination to follow it through. Virtue depends on character and character is learned by example (i.e., it flows from a desire to emulate others). These imply that Christians in finance are called both to remain in their institutions and to be "salt and light" to others by the virtues they display. Virtues cannot be relied on alone, but a system that neither promotes nor rewards such virtue sows the seeds of its own destruction.

Meanwhile, by appealing to banks to acquire "public responsibility" and "moral vision," we attribute agency to an institution, something we ourselves have created. This risks becoming idolatry. It can also become a way for individuals to seek to avoid responsibility by blaming the system or the institution when there were alternative choices that such individuals could have made.

The size of the financial sector should be scrutinized, both from the standpoint of financial stability and its moral implications, as should the monopoly power of large banks. Personal relationships must again become core to financial transactions.

CHAPTER 4: THE HOUSEHOLD SECTOR—PRIVATE DEBT

4.1 Economics Perspective

While bankers must bear some of the responsibility for household indebtedness, especially for the over-marketing and selling of financial products, individuals were not obliged to take on massive debt burdens. Consumers were complicit in the process of over-lending, celebrating the house price rise and consumer boom up to 2007.

The conventional life cycle paradigm of economics has households borrowing early in adulthood to buy homes, then saving in middle age to accumulate wealth for retirement. In this context, both borrowing and saving appropriately are seen as sensible behavior. However, economists also recognize—albeit without satisfactory explanation—that many people are "myopically" unwilling to save for the future, and borrow excessively in relation to their incomes. Such borrowing tends to enable them both to consume more than they earn in the present, and to buy properties beyond their means.

The current "profligate" cohort in the US and UK appears unusually affected by this tendency to low saving and excessive borrowing, which may be highly damaging in the long term, particularly for their income in retirement. This pattern is not observed in most European Union countries, where saving is much higher and borrowing much lower. There is also a shorter-term downside to the free availability of debt, especially when people borrow at excessive loan-to-value ratios. Principally the risk is of default. But even if consumers are able and willing to repay debt, shocks to income or rises in interest rates can lead to stress on family budgets and relationships.

While economics offers an understanding of the behavior of households in the recent crisis, it does not answer the question why people acted contrary to their own interests, just to consume more "now."   → nee, Moral Hazzard ⇒ gov't bail outs
Hedonism

4.2 Theological Perspective

Debt has assumed undue proportions, as wealth and consumption have become central to human life and well-being, rather than kingdom values such as the quality of relationships with others and with God. However, the irrationality of recent consumer behavior is unsurprising, since a generation that increasingly disowns its creator is not likely to act in its own interests either.

The Bible's warnings about debt include the way it limits the flexibility we have in life and can lead to a form of slavery. There is a biblical parallel of debt to sin, given that both are enslaving and destructive.

In the Bible, there are widespread provisions for writing off debt, but they typically assume the borrower is poor and the loan a virtual obligation owing to adverse financial circumstances. They are much less applicable in cases of voluntary transactions motivated by desire for a higher living standard, as we have seen in recent years. In that case, the Bible encourages responsibility for actions; there is an obligation on borrowers to repay debts incurred and to avoid assistance if it lies within our means. Individuals should not walk away from their debts via "strategic default," in other words. Equally, lenders should lend with restraint and be willing to extend terms in case of difficulty.

A wider obligation rests on all Christians to care mercifully and generously for the needy, who cannot sustain consumption due to shocks to income or following their own financial errors. Christians are commanded to give to those who have immediate acute needs, such as hunger or lack of clothing and shelter.

4.3 Ways Forward

Access to credit is essential to household welfare, and the issue is whether it can be distributed with less risk of financial distress for households.

Mortgage lenders and their regulators must control loan-to-value or loan-to-income ratios to reduce risk. But equally justice suggests greater taxation of housing and/or an easing of restrictions on supply of land may be needed, at least in the UK, to prevent houses being priced out of the reach of those on low income.

Consumer lenders actively encouraged the buildup of debt, advertising heavily amongst the poor where the greatest margins are, behavior redolent of biblical usury. Ways to tackle this could include a cap on interest rates, credit card maxima linked to income, or restrictions on advertising for consumer credit.

The church has a clear role to play as offering an alternative kingdom culture to that of debt and consumption. It should seek to shift social perceptions towards a "save-first" view. If individuals were reintroduced to the benefits of saving to buy goods, they would be much more willing and able to save for their own retirement. Equally, Christians need to consider whether they have been absorbed by a consumer-oriented society, while the church must show mercy by offering support for those who are weak and vulnerable owing to debt problems.

CHAPTER 5: THE GOVERNMENT SECTOR—PUBLIC DEBT

5.1 Economic Perspective

Economists distinguish between cyclical and structural fiscal deficits, where the latter are persistent even when the economy regains its normal or "trend" rate of growth. Cyclical deficits can be an optimal response to recessions, buoying the economy when demand falls. In a crisis, recapitalization of banks entails a steep rise in the level of public debt, and this has sharply worsened public finances. However, many economists argue that the fiscal crisis now faced in the US and UK also reflects a structural deficit that had been sustained in the previous boom, as the government spent more than it could expect in tax revenue even during a time of buoyant economic activity.

5.2 Theological Perspective

Biblical teaching states that the government should be supported by citizens as instituted by God to be a source of stability. There are theological reasons to help the poor that apply to government as well as to individuals, and these imply some form of welfare system and taxation, correcting some of the grosser inequalities that would be generated by the free market.

This does not imply a need to run structural fiscal deficits on average over the cycle. Rather, biblical prudence would suggest balancing the books over the cycle, while running deficits for stabilization purposes during recessions. A crucial downside of the current growth in debt is that future generations of taxpayers will be obliged to finance what can be seen as errors by the government, bankers, and borrowers of today.

5.3 *Ways Forward*

Underlying the occurrence of structural fiscal deficits is a willingness of governments, for electoral reasons, not to levy sufficient tax to fully finance public expenditures. Furthermore, by boosting growth, structural deficits mislead people into going into debt, by leading them to believe their income growth—and house price appreciation—will continue to be high. Promotion of student debt by governments in the US, and more recently in the UK, "conditions" people to expect to be in debt all of their lives, weakening their resistance to credit card advertising or unwise mortgage borrowing.

There is a need for governments to improve regulation so that bank rescues are made less likely in future, but equally that fiscal policy should be responsible. Furthermore, governments have a responsibility to warn the population when economic conditions resemble previous crisis run-ups (like 1988–90). Like banks, the public cannot treat the government as something autonomous. Rather, the public has a responsibility to understand these issues, take a view, and press for it in public and via their elected representatives. And we must stand in accusation when we discover we have been misled.

CHAPTER 6: CONCLUSIONS AND RECOMMENDATIONS

Blame for the current situation is not attributable solely to bankers—households and governments also bear a share of responsibility. All three sought to maximize their personal benefit in the pursuit of self-interest, showing greed, selfishness, and impatience, which was ultimately counterproductive. This led to catastrophe for many: beyond those directly responsible, casualties include not only those unemployed due to the crisis but also the coming generation. They are burdened with future taxes to pay off government debt and required to finance future pensions against a background of worsening demographics. They also face ever-heavier costs of a university education, and, notably in the UK, are priced out of the residential property market.

Conventional bank regulation is part of the answer to preventing recurrence of the crisis, but encouragement and enforcement of virtues in banking is also essential. Relationships need to be reestablished as critical to generating a stable and socially beneficial financial system.

The underlying social pressure for ever-more consumption needs to be tempered for our own long-term self-interest, the benefit of wider society, and for environmental reasons. And governments need to recognize the benefits of restraining average public spending to be in line with tax revenue.

A biblical analysis of the current situation implies that idolatry in economics needs to be recognized and the structural injustices it generates condemned—we are all responsible for opposing them. The analysis of this book presents a critique of the overall aims of economics —wealth, consumption, and power—in contrast to Jesus' proclamation of the kingdom of God, the law of love for God and neighbor, and responsible stewardship of resources. The church is called to broadcast the virtues of the biblical approach energetically.

Chapter 1

Events of the Financial Crisis

The crisis, in a generic sense, was not an unusual event (see Appendix 1). As has been the case for many other crises of recent decades,[1] it was preceded by growing vulnerability of the global economic and financial system to shocks in the form of a credit boom, untested financial innovations, increasing indebtedness of financial institutions, risk taking, and the formation of an asset price bubble. This makes it surprising that it was not better forecast.[2]

That said, there were some idiosyncratic features. Since a major asset price bubble and the riskiest lending were in US housing, sub-prime related debt was its proximate cause. The size, global integration, and complexity of the US financial markets made it inevitable that the crisis would become global. And high household debt in countries such as the UK, Ireland, Iceland, and Spain, as well as even bigger bubbles in housing and fragile financial institutions, made their economies also highly vulnerable. As a baseline for the overall analysis of the book, an outline of key features of the crisis from an economic point of view follows. Those already familiar should proceed to chapter 2.[3]

1. See Davis (1995), Davis and Karim (2009), and Reinhart and Rogoff (2009).

2. See Davis and Karim (2008) for an assessment of the degree to which the crisis was forecast by major UK and international financial organizations.

3. See Barrell and Davis (2008) and IMF (2008) for more detail.

GLOBAL INTEREST RATES OVER 2000–2007 WERE LOW

One reason for the boom that preceded the crisis was high levels of "global liquidity." Countries such as China, Japan, and Korea, which were saving more than they invested at home, built up current account surpluses and foreign exchange reserves. In effect, such countries lent money on a massive scale to deficit countries like the US and UK. As a result of such a flood of global liquidity, global real (inflation-adjusted) interest rates fell after 2001 and long-term real rates were probably 1 percentage point below their level of the previous decade. There were also low short-term real interest rates arising from the easy monetary policy in countries such as the US. These low interest rates were naturally reflected in low interest rates for loans, making them attractive to borrowers.

A LENDING AND ASSET PRICE BOOM TOOK PLACE OVER 2000–2007

In this environment of cheap credit, lending grew at unprecedented rates, especially in countries like the US, the UK, Iceland, Ireland, and Spain. Part of the growth in lending was to types of borrowers (such as sub-prime[4] and buy-to-let borrowers) that had been previously excluded or rationed in access to mortgage credit, due to the high level of default risk they pose to the lender. These types of borrowers were offered large amounts of credit, especially in the US, and to a lesser extent in the UK. Some borrowers falsified their incomes to get more credit. More creditworthy borrowers also increased their debts markedly,

---

4. Note that sub-prime refers to the credit quality of the mortgage, not to the amount loaned or the status of the borrower. Hence, although many such loans were indeed to the previously "financially excluded" it is also perfectly possible, and was commonplace, for loans to be made on sub-prime terms to middle- to upper-income families to buy homes for up to $1 million in value; also much sub-prime lending was re-mortgaging (Ferguson [2009], 265–75). Some commentators argue that the US government bears partial responsibility for the growth in sub-prime (1) due to the provisions of the Community Reinvestment Act of 1977, which mandates banks to make a proportion of loans to low-income borrowers, and (2) owing to the regulation of the government-sponsored agencies Fanny Mae and Freddy Mac by the Department of Housing and Urban Development, which mandated those agencies to buy increasing proportions of securitizations backed by sub-prime loans.

sometimes to buy new homes but often also to release equity from their homes for consumption purposes. No doubt partly driven by release of credit constraints, real house prices in the US and the UK rose far above their longer-term trend. House prices became similarly overvalued in countries such as Ireland, Iceland, and Spain.

POLICY ERRORS WERE COMMITTED

Low short-term interest rates in the US were initially a response to the equity price collapse of 2000–2003, whose feared deflationary impact they sought to counteract. But it can be argued that the equity price fall was soon more than offset by the above-mentioned debt-financed housing boom, which gathered strength as equity prices recovered in 2003–4. The credit and housing boom was hence not counteracted by monetary policy that stayed "too loose for too long," especially in the US. Although there were warnings by central banks and international organizations of risks of a financial crisis resulting from the debt and asset price boom, very little was done beyond cautionary speeches by Central Bank Governors (so-called moral suasion) to counter the boom. Monetary policy was not tightened until the boom was far advanced, and bank regulation did not counteract the growing risks banks were running. Fiscal policy was also loose, as will be discussed further in chapter 5.

THERE WAS WIDESPREAD FINANCIAL INNOVATION, SPECULATION, AND EASY LENDING BY BANKS

Low interest rates prompted a "hunt for yield" on the part of global banks and institutional investors, as both they themselves and their savers sought a reasonable return on their assets. In this context, high-yielding financial innovations such as asset-backed securities (ABS)[5] became popular as a source of profit for banks. ABS are basically a means whereby banks making loans can package them and sell them to investors as bonds, a process known as securitization. While

---

5. We use the term ABS also to refer to collateralized debt obligations (CDOs), which are basically securities formed from individual ABS. There were also CDO-squared which were CDOs made of other CDOs. The more complex the product, the more difficult it was to find out what assets were actually backing them.

us Federal subsidies for housing was the key error - Fannie + Freddie publicly guaranteed ABS had long been a feature of the US financial system, the 2000s saw an unprecedented boom in private ABS.

In issuing ABS, lender banks would profit from up-front fees for loans (such as those to sub-prime borrowers) without having to hold the loan on the balance sheet. Any type of loan seemed to be suitable for securitization in the 2000–2007 period, and especially sub-prime loans (i.e., loans to borrowers of low credit quality). The ABS that were most central to the crisis have the interesting property that, with a modicum of diversification and so-called credit enhancement, a bunch of poor quality loans can be made (or seem to be made) into mostly top quality securities.[6] It's as if lead can be made into 80 percent gold and 20 percent plutonium-nuclear waste. The math seemed to be correct, but, of course, in practice such "financial alchemy" was not feasible and lead remained lead.

There was a further "twist" in that securitization reduces the incentive of lender banks to assess loans for credit quality, since the ABS holder would take the risk of default. This helps explain the risky loans to sub-prime, buy-to-let, etc., borrowers that were made during the boom—the lender bank did not bear the risk. Some such loans were actually known as "liar loans" because the lending officer at the bank would induce the client to exaggerate his or her income so as to get a larger loan.

Global banks also made their own balance sheets more risky in the search for profit (see Appendix 2). They reduced their liquid assets, given low interest rates that could be earned on them, leaving them with less cover for any emergency needs for finance. They grew their balance sheets via aggressive wholesale liability management (i.e., borrowing from other banks and money markets rather than retail depositors). Furthermore, they both invested in ABS themselves and shifted such securitized assets to off-balance-sheet vehicles called conduits and special investment vehicles (SIVs), in order to avoid regulatory capital requirements (see Appendix 2 for further clarification). So paradoxically, while they knew that *their own* loans backing ABS were substandard,

---

6. Credit enhancement in general is a method whereby the lender is provided with reassurance that the borrower will honor the obligation to repay debt. This is undertaken through additional collateral, insurance, or a third party guarantee. It is considered to reduce default risk, thereby increasing the overall credit rating and lowering interest rates.

they were willing to give the benefit of the doubt to loans backing *other banks'* ABS. But, of course, they were also substandard—typically 20 percent gold and 80 percent plutonium-nuclear waste.

It is clear that banks took on more credit risk than they otherwise would, particularly via ABS but also in more usual balance sheet lending, notably to commercial property projects. Banks and others may have simply forgotten the last crisis they had experienced, as well as considering themselves "too big to fail" (i.e., supposing that national governments would support them if they got into difficulties). Other reasons may include the scope for securitization and the impression of liquidity it gave, high credit ratings, and yields on ABS, and the seeming precision of risk models based on inadequate data. Accordingly, the impact of risky loans on the loan portfolio was considered to be offset by safe ABS. All this despite the fact the ABS were extremely difficult to understand and had not been tested in a downturn—like drugs whose side effects are unknown but which are marketed anyway.

The crisis in fact showed that the risk models for the ABS were flawed and did not allow for the possibility of US house prices falling nationwide as they did. It also showed the gross errors in assessments by the rating agencies, which stated that the "gold" ABS bonds were almost risk free. Rating agencies, being paid by the issuer, were widely suspected of offering unduly lenient ratings to ABS.

NUMEROUS TAKEOVERS OCCURRED IN BANKING AND FINANCE

The boom in lending, asset prices, and innovation was accompanied by a peak in mergers and acquisitions in the financial sector, with the takeover of the Dutch bank ABN-AMRO by Royal Bank of Scotland being a typical example. Such takeovers were later to ensnare the buyers, given the debt they had incurred for the transaction, as was also the case for Lehman Brothers' purchase of the property company Archstone in 2007.

THERE WAS A COLLAPSE IN CONFIDENCE AND ASSET PRICES, LEADING TO LOSSES FOR BANKS

2007 saw growing realization of potential losses on sub-prime mortgages as US house prices fell and defaults increased. As early as October 2008, the IMF[7] estimated such losses as $1.4 *trillion*. These losses, along with uncertainty and the sudden realization that banks did not understand the properties of the ABS, combined to generate sales of ABS on international markets. Sales led, in turn, not just to price falls but also market liquidity failure. In other words, *the ABS bonds could not be sold at any price*. Since banks hold a proportion of their securities at so-called mark-to-market pricing, they made immediate losses[8] as prices of ABS went into free fall while the assets themselves could not be disposed of. Effects were felt not only by US banks but also by European banks that had bought ABS of sub-prime loans. Meanwhile, bank conduits and SIVs could no longer obtain financing from wholesale money markets, which meant sponsoring banks had to take the often-"toxic" ABS assets they held back on their balance sheets, thus aggravating the situation for the banks.

FREEZING OF SECURITIZATION AND INTERBANK FUNDING ENSUED

By late 2007, banks were unable to securitize the mortgages and other loans they were issuing, owing to liquidity collapse of the ABS market. They also experienced calls on backup lines of credit for conduits and SIVs. Accordingly, the banks "hoarded liquidity" in order to provide sufficient funding for their ongoing business. This hoarding was also motivated by the fear that other banks they might lend to on the interbank market might bear undisclosed losses on ABS. So, interbank funding began to be withdrawn—an unprecedented event in the domestic markets of the advanced industrial countries. Other forms of wholesale credit also became hard to obtain. Banks in general were vulnerable to financial distress due to reduced wholesale and interbank funding owing to their low holdings of liquid assets,

---

7. IMF (2008).

8. This was unlike banking crises in the past where loans have typically been held on balance sheet at historic cost with no specific price. Banks were hit far quicker.

growth in reliance on short-term wholesale funding, and dependence on securitization.

In the wake of this, banks sought to reduce balance sheet lending, at the same time that house price falls rendered borrowers cautious, leading to unprecedented falls in mortgage lending as well as lending to corporations. The ongoing process unleashed by the crisis can be referred to as "deleveraging,"[9] as banks and other institutions sought to reduce exposure to high-risk sectors, selling assets or reducing asset growth, as well as reducing dependence on unstable wholesale funding and rebuilding capital adequacy. The process was accelerated by the ongoing fall in asset prices and the rise in private sector defaults on loans, as well as by closure of securitization markets. Central banks offered massive volumes of liquidity to prevent bank failures and sought in vain to restart the interbank funding markets.

BANK FAILURES TOOK PLACE

An early consequence of the collapse of wholesale funding markets was the failure of the apparently solvent UK mortgage bank Northern Rock, which had an aggressive wholesale funding ratio and had been relying on securitizing assets, which was no longer feasible.[10] It suffered "runs" in both wholesale and retail markets (see Appendix 2 for a discussion of "bank runs" and the fragility of banks in periods of crisis). Beyond Northern Rock, failures in 2007 included mainly two small German banks. The casualties of this ongoing pattern in 2008 were much more important. Up to September 2008, they included the US firms Bear Stearns (taken over with government guarantees), IndyMac (failed), and the quasi-public agencies Fanny Mae and Freddy Mac (effectively nationalized).

By September 2008 it seemed that the crisis was ongoing, but not worsening. But following the bankruptcy of the major US investment bank Lehman Brothers (unsupported by the authorities) in mid-September there was a sharp worsening of market conditions. Whereas the direct cause of failure of Lehmans was losses on low-rated securities they had been unable to sell, there was also evidence of persistent

9. IMF (2008).

10. On the Northern Rock Crisis, see UK Treasury Committee (2008).

masking of the firm's adverse financial position.[11] As institutions and investors tried to unwind their positions, and fear of default by counterparties to transactions increased, the market became disorderly and panic took hold.

Money market funds in the US made such large losses that their ability to maintain a constant selling price was put into question, leading to panic sales by investors akin to bank runs.[12] The equity market, which had been surprisingly little affected by the crisis up to that point, began to fall sharply. This particularly reflected low confidence in banks that were dependent on wholesale funding, because wholesale funding markets, that had previously been costly and restrictive, proved to be totally closed to such institutions after Lehmans' failure. Cross border lending was even more sharply curtailed than domestic.

THERE WERE FISCAL INJECTIONS AND "LENDER OF LAST RESORT" ASSISTANCE TO SAVE FAILING BANKS

The authorities acted in the wake of the worsening of market conditions. Provision of liquidity by central banks to the markets increased further. The US authorities suggested and passed the Paulson plan (called the TARP or Troubled Asset Relief Program), which was designed to restore liquidity to the markets by using $700 billion to buy up ABS. However, this plan did not address the solvency of the banks directly and left many banks exposed. The American Insurance Group (AIG) suffered insolvency.[13] It, closely followed by Bradford

11. This practice was a type of repurchase agreement that temporarily removed securities from the company's balance sheet at the time of financial reporting. However, unlike typical repurchase agreements, these deals were described by Lehman as the outright sale of securities and created "a materially misleading picture of the firm's financial condition in late 2007 and 2008," according to the 2010 report by a court-appointed examiner.

12. Cutting the selling price below $1 is called "breaking the buck" and would tend to cause panic among money market fund investors, who expected such funds to be ultra safe.

13. Technically, AIG had acted as credit protection seller under credit default swaps (CDSs). Under the terms of those CDSs it did not have to post any collateral because of its own good credit rating. It suffered a ratings downgrade, as default rates rose on the CDSs, which in turn triggered the requirement to post collateral. Then AIG could not liquidate sufficient assets to meet the collateral requirements and accordingly went bankrupt: see FSA (2009), 27.

and Bingley in the UK, had to be nationalized. Merrill Lynch and Wachovia were taken over. Washington Mutual was closed by regulators and sold to JPMorgan Chase. The remaining US investment banks had to become bank holding companies. Banks dependent on cross border financing were hardest hit. For example, the two major Belgian banks had to be nationalized and all three Icelandic banks, in which many UK and Dutch savers had been induced to invest with high deposit rates, failed in October 2008.

Significant public sector stakes totaling £37 billion were taken in three major lenders in the UK—HBOS, RBS, and Lloyds—in order to ensure their solvency. Guarantees were offered for their liabilities and the Bank of England expanded its swap facility for illiquid assets. HBOS in particular seemed close to failure, owing to a huge rise in loan defaults and a reliance on wholesale funding, until it was announced that a takeover by Lloyds would occur. The effective nationalization of a large part of the UK banking sector ensured that this system would remain solvent, and a number of European countries announced that they would also strengthen the equity base of banks by taking a public share.

The TARP was redirected to the same purpose, and in mid-October 2008, $250 billion was made available to US banks to increase their capital adequacy ratios, with the government buying shares in them. Citigroup, for example, benefited from two capital injections in quick succession and Bank of America also required two rounds of support. General Motors and Chrysler, two of the three major US carmakers, also received support from the TARP. Countries in the Euro area, as well as Switzerland and Sweden, also announced recapitalizations, for example amounting to 41 billion euros for France and 130 billion euros for Germany.

Going beyond recapitalization, the US Treasury temporarily stepped in to guarantee the value of money fund shares at a minimum value of $1, markedly extending the "safety net" of public support for the financial system. Some fiscal authorities set out to guarantee wholesale liabilities, covering money market borrowing and term debt. In the US, these guarantees were estimated by the Bank of England to be worth $1,400 billion.[14] The UK authorities offered guarantees of

14. Bank of England (2008).

bank liabilities up to three years' maturity amounting to £250 billion for banks seen as adequately capitalized.

Having cut interest rates to the bone, the US Fed bought a variety of nontraditional assets such as mortgage backed securities, commercial paper, and ABS to seek to support economic activity. Both the Fed and the Bank of England in due course bought government bonds under the guise of "quantitative easing" to further ease monetary conditions, a process that in effect "prints money."

EFFECTS ON THE REAL ECONOMY WERE SEVERE

In 2008–9, the real economies of most advanced countries were badly affected, with deep recessions, falling house prices, and rising unemployment. At the time of writing there is evidence of weak recovery, but prospects for return to previous growth rates and levels of employment seem remote and the eurozone crisis threatens to cause a "double dip" global recession.

There has been widespread default on the heavy mortgage debt that households have incurred, with, for example, 2,037,000 US households entering foreclosure in 2009 and 1,845,000 in 2010, compared with only 762,000 in the boom year 2006.[15] Further defaults may be expected as house prices remain low and rates continue to rise above the initial "teaser" rates. Meanwhile in the UK 135,000 individuals went bankrupt in both 2009 and 2010 compared with 68,000 in 2005.

Even if households do not default on mortgages and consumer credit (due, for example, to unemployment), their consumption cannot grow at the rates seen in the past few years, given the burden of interest payments and the lack of availability of loans to "extract equity." This is a further aspect of the long and painful process of "deleveraging" as households, financial institutions, and some businesses restrict expenditures over time to return to sustainable levels of indebtedness.

Another concern relates to the enormous volume of public debt that has been incurred, not only due to the bank rescues but because a sharp recession reduces tax revenue while increasing need for benefit payments, and governments have also carried out discretionary fiscal

15. Source: Credit Conditions Report for May 2011, Federal Reserve Bank of New York.

loosening. Funding difficulties for Greece, Ireland, and Portugal have necessitated rescues by other Euro area members and at the time of writing threaten the stability of the single currency itself.

Emerging markets countries were also, for a time in 2008–9, badly affected[16] as trade finance and external finance became much harder to obtain. However, in the end they were less hard hit than advanced industrial economies. Indeed, some commentators see the relative resilience of economies such as China and India as indicative of a broader shift in economic power and influence away from the advanced industrial countries.

Policy issues still facing the authorities in the US, UK, and other advanced countries include how long to maintain loose monetary policies, how rapidly to tighten fiscal policy, and how to tighten global and domestic bank regulation so the crisis does not recur.[17]

16. IMF (2008).

17. See Basel Committee (2011) for proposals at the time of writing.

Chapter 2

Comparing the View of Humankind from Economics and Theology

Having outlined the events of the crisis, we now examine key issues raised by the crisis in the light of economics and biblical theology. We contend that economics is the "ruling paradigm" in today's society and government, and therefore it is appropriate to combine its insights with those of biblical theology, rather than focusing solely on the latter. In doing so, we are following what scholars call the "Wisdom tradition" of the Bible, and indeed much of the biblical material we will use is derived from the Wisdom books, such as Proverbs. Israel's Wisdom tradition can be seen as her distinctive participation in the broader academic culture of the day—Egypt and the nations around had comparable Wisdom traditions.

So, in the same vein, a critical dialogue between biblical theology and secular modes of understanding, such as economics, is biblically appropriate. John Goldingay talks of the book of Proverbs as part of an intellectual quest *shared* with peoples of non-Israelite cultures: "Much of Proverbs is comparable with the teaching of other peoples and seems to have learned from it."[1] Yet he also writes of the need for a *critical distinctiveness* to biblically based Wisdom—"reverence for God

1. Goldingay (2006), 582.

or submission to God is of key significance if we want to be people of insight."[2] In the same way, in seeking to understand the "signs of the times," Christians need to learn from, and gratefully share insights with, secular learning. Yet, at the same time, Christians must engage in a critical dialogue, such as the one in this book, that challenges that secular wisdom with the fundamental kingdom truth of the gospel.

Considering views of economics among secular and Christian commentators, Hobsbawm states, "economics, though subject to the requirements of logic and consistency, has flourished as a form of theology—probably in the Western world, the most influential branch of secular theology,"[3] while Nelson states that it "offers a set of principles and understandings that give meaning to, define a purpose for, and significantly frame the perception of human existence."[4] Britton and Sedgwick, in a Christian analysis of economics, point out that there is "not much in economics that can be demonstrated beyond reasonable doubt" even though it is an "impressive body of reasoning, extremely influential in contemporary culture, providing one type of insight into the way modern society works."[5] Hence, there is all the more reason to consider it alongside theology.

Certainly, economics' influence extends well beyond academia, because it is widely taught to those active in business and management, and also pervades political debates on economic policy. There have been "missionaries" taking the ideas of free market economics to the developing world. IMF financial support for countries in difficulty and related structural adjustment programs have widely been seen as having a similar effect. Collier attacks "economism," the tendency to give primacy to economics over other sources of meaning and value.[6] Accordingly, we set out in the next section a basic understanding of the nature of economic thinking, in relation to humanity *per se*. For a deeper analysis see Hay[7] and Britton and Sedgwick.[8] Note

---

2. Ibid., 581.

3. Hobsbawm (1994), quoted in Britton and Sedgwick (2003), 9.

4. Nelson (1991), quoted in Britton and Sedgwick (2003), 9.

5. Britton and Sedgwick (2003), 292.

6. Collier (1992), quoted in ibid., 12.

7. Hay (1989).

8. Britton and Sedgwick (2003).

that we focus on the leading approach to economics known as the "neoclassical" paradigm.[9]

2.1 ECONOMICS—TODAY'S RULING PARADIGM

Economics, like other social sciences, differs from the physical sciences in that the unit of observation is the behavior of the human being. Hence, as noted by Hay,[10] economists do not merely analyze using detached observation (thus deducing cause and effect) but can use introspection (how would *I* act in these circumstances?). Weighing up alternatives and making a decision is core to the way economists think and develop hypotheses in the light of their wider understanding of human economic activity. For example, "I bought this house because prices are rising; I borrowed a great deal because interest rates are low at present." Accordingly, human actions are understood in terms of reasons, preferences, and motives, and not simply cause and effect. Indeed, often the methodology of economics is not one of scientific experiment to test a hypothesis but of assumptions about behavior and motivation, which are not subject to empirical test.

We can contrast the "positive" economic domain (analysis of what *does* happen) with the "normative" (what *should* happen), dealing with positive first. As noted by Britton and Sedgwick, economics is inevitably normative as well as positive, because values cannot be readily separated from facts when human nature is the subject matter.[11]

Positive Economics

Positive economics typically uses a simplified concept of mankind, often called "rational economic *humanity*." This concept is assumed to be generally applicable across the human race, irrespective of cultural differences. At a basic level, individuals operate in an environment of scarcity and competition. They are assumed to have preferences

9. This is the dominant approach for both academics and economic policymakers; there exist alternatives such as Marxian economics, which talks, for example, of poverty as arising from the exploitative alienation of workers from the product of their labor; see Griffin and Gurley (1985), 1089.

10. Hay (1989), 101.

11. Britton and Sedgwick (2003), 42.

concerning the set of consequences of all their possible actions, be they consumption, labor supply, or investment. These preferences are rational in three senses. First, they are "complete" in that for all pairs of choices, the person either prefers one or is indifferent between them. Second, preferences are "transitive," so if we prefer A to B and B to C, we prefer A to C also. Third, individuals (on average) act "rationally" in accordance with these preferences, in the sense that given a set of available actions, there is no action available to them superior in consequences to the action they have chosen. Often there is added the idea of "non-satiation," meaning that *more* of a good is always preferred to less.

As noted by Britton and Sedgwick, the veracity of these forms of rationality are articles of *faith* for they are not logically necessary, self-evident, or obvious.[12] A variant on the theory of preference is "revealed preference" theory that applies this approach directly to analysis of actual choices between a set of goods, services, assets, employment, use of time, etc., thus avoiding the need to consider what people's decision processes are (albeit usually assuming they are as described above).

The basis of the approach of "rational economic humanity" is the utilitarianism of the Victorian philosophers Jeremy Bentham (1748–1832) and John Stuart Mill (1806–73), who saw experiences as generating pleasure or pain, desirable or undesirable feelings.[13] So, individuals rationally seek to increase desirable feelings and reduce undesirable ones. As noted by Hay, according to a utilitarian, the goal of an individual is to "promote his own interests, preserve his own life, increase his own pleasures, and diminish his pains."[14] Then, the calculation could be simply summarized as a single measure of utility that human beings seek rationally to maximize. Nineteenth-century economists such as Francis Edgeworth (1845–1926) took this approach to mean that individuals are motivated "only by self-interest."[15] The

12. Britton and Sedgwick (2003), 42

13. See for example Mill (1836).

14. Hay (1989), 105.

15. In fact although classical utilitarians would argue that such a pursuit of self-interest is correct as a psychological ("positive") proposition, they did not rule out individuals taking into account in their ethical ("normative") decisions the interests of others, as summarized in the phrase "the greatest happiness for the greatest

main development since then has been a focus on ordering of preferences rather than absolute levels of utility that could be measured by
an outside observer. Corollaries are that *only consequences count*, not
the actions themselves; actions are evaluated for their effects without
reference to rules of conduct.

Meanwhile, everything except self-interest is typically excluded as a motive in economic behavior (this is what economists call
"hedonism"[16]). This is not a *necessary* feature of the subject. Economists
could include other motives besides self-interest in analyzing human
behavior in terms of "utility" (e.g., others' consumption, such as that
of the poorest in society, as well as one's own could enter preferences),
but they typically do not do so, except in certain specialized research
articles. Economists assume that pursuit of self-interest is a "useful
simplification," which is broadly correct on average. This has consequences that go wider than economic theory, reaching into politics
and society at large. Maximizing one's own consumption less disutility of labor or, as an entrepreneur, maximizing profits is, in this view,
often widely seen as the "*only* rational approach" to life, particularly
since the Reagan/Thatcher years of deregulation of the 1980s.

By seeing individuals as individualistically selfish in their behavior, economic theory tends to rule out intrinsic value to community life, beyond the benefit the *individual* may obtain from it.
Relationships, beyond those pursued for self-interested motives, also
have little role to play. Ethical goals such as poverty relief are blanked
out beyond their impact on the well-being of individuals. By assuming individual self-interest, economics could be seen as recognizing
the ubiquity of fallen human behavior. Indeed, some economists such
as Becker have argued from evolutionary biology that evolution will
eliminate those genetic characteristics inconsistent with self-interest
and survival.[17] Those not following self-interest and survival single-
mindedly will fail to pass on their genes, in the same way that a firm

---

number." The latter is also a feature of normative economics, which we discuss in
the section below.

16. It might technically be called "egoistic hedonism" since it assumes that the
individual take only their own happiness or pleasure into account in their decisions.

17. See, for example, Rayo and Becker (2007).

that does not maximize profits will be eliminated from the market by competitors.

Since the individual is usually assumed to be selfish rather than altruistic, charitable giving is hard for economics to understand.[18] Whereas the possibility of perfect altruism is conceded (i.e., the individual cares only about the benefit to the recipient), economists feel there is more evidence for explanations highlighting a "warm glow" (i.e., some additional inner satisfaction from giving) or "prestige" (valuing recognition by others for giving, along the lines of Jesus' critique of the Pharisees in Matthew 6:2: "So when you give to the needy, do not announce it with trumpets, as the hypocrites do in the synagogues and on the streets, to be honored by men. I tell you the truth, they have received their reward in full."). The test of the "warm glow" or "prestige" is that private giving does not decline one-for-one with government giving to the same recipient—which has been empirically verified.

There have been a number of criticisms of the "rational economic humanity" paradigm from a "commonsense" point of view, even abstracting from a theological critique.

- First, following rules of conduct may have value in itself, both to the individual and wider society, implying a value to *actions* and not just consequences. Moral norms that have a major effect on human behavior should not be omitted or just included as "tastes."

- Second, a pure hedonist who focuses only on current pleasures might make no provision for the future, only the present, and this is thought to be unrealistic (although we see elements of such myopia in current household behavior discussed in chapter 4).

- Third, the "rational economic humanity" paradigm omits the concept of "commitment," where people choose to act in a certain way regardless of the effect on their utility. For example, agreeing to provision of goods to the community that one benefits little from, repaying a debt, or continuing in a marriage.

- Fourth, it is evident that humans value community links.

18. See Hernández-Murillo and Roisman (2005).

We note, however, that these objections have weakened since the 1960s as rules and commitment have been seen as obstructions to self-fulfillment and hedonism has been celebrated. Community links have weakened also. The paradigm, on this basis, may be coming closer to the truth.

A more technical objection is that individuals do not have the information to make rational decisions in the way described. Advertising (e.g., for consumer credit) influences individuals well beyond provision of information—it shapes preferences themselves and generates peer group pressure. Furthermore, it can be argued that people might try to get to a *satisfactory* level of utility, perhaps repeating or copying earlier decisions, rather than maximizing it, not least due to a lack of complete information or a desire to keep options open. But economists typically continue to use the standard full-information rational paradigm.

Normative Economics

The normative approach in economics traces the consequences of free choice by rational individuals for society. It typically does not make prescriptions about individual ethics, but gives advice to policymakers on *public* choices.

It is also pervaded by utilitarianism, in that it typically states that a social situation is superior if individual well-being is greater, where the latter is something the individual seeks to maximize. Accordingly, a traditional approach is to say that the best choice for society is one that maximizes the sum of such happiness. In principle, such well-being or happiness is not just material pleasure or pain but also could include nonmaterial or spiritual elements in life. But this is usually not taken to be the case. Again, preferences for equality in society, for instance, can be included so that individuals with less well-being have a greater weight. However, such additive or cardinal utility is widely criticized and instead economists prefer to consider relative utility. The key concept is *Pareto optimality*, stating that social welfare is and should be increased if someone could be made better off without another being worse off. This only requires a ranking of individual outcomes.

Using this tool, as discussed in Davis, economics assumes that the pursuit of self-interest will lead to an optimal outcome for all (the "competitive equilibrium") across the economy as a whole.[19] This is achieved by everyone acting in a self-interested manner, as noted by Adam Smith: "It is not from the benevolence of the butcher, the brewer, or the baker that we expect our dinner, but from their regard to their own interest."[20] The process of reaching an optimum via markets is often called the operation of Adam Smith's "invisible hand."

In more detail, the standard "neoclassical" economic paradigm is the "competitive equilibrium." It starts with an initial set of asset-endowments for individuals (talents, skills, capital), who pursue their own self-interest. It then states that financial, labor, and product markets will operate to set prices so that all supplies and demands balance, and no one could be made better off without another being worse off (Pareto optimality). This will be the case if certain conditions are fulfilled, notably, that there are no monopolistic producers or traders who can control prices independently of the market.

These assumptions, and the "optimal" outcome they generate, naturally lead to support for laissez-faire policies and opposition to any government intervention to redistribute wealth. An example of the laissez-faire approach is the so-called minimal state that just ensures the rule of law and defense, and possibly infrastructure. Individuals following this line of argument tend to see a more active state as a threat to freedom as well as to prosperity. They may argue that the poor will benefit from "trickle-down" effects of growth without any positive measures to help them. They are also suspicious of regulation of markets, other than that against monopolies, urging that the system is self-correcting. The financial crisis has, of course, cast doubt on the last-mentioned suggestion.

The most laissez-faire economists even view individual rights and justice with suspicion, as they may violate the competitive equilibrium and are typically omitted from calculations of utility maximization. But rights and justice come closer to the "commonsense" view that a person has dignity and individual value, and should be treated as a subject and not an object. For example, a "social contract" in political theory may specify that governments should ensure all citizens have sufficient resources to cover their basic needs (nutrition, shelter,

19. Davis (2007), 14.
20. Smith (1776), Book 1, chapter 2.

sanitation, health care), basic education, and also political liberty, which in turn empowers the poor to participate in wealth creation in a self-directed manner.

Rawls, for example, talks about justice as requiring, on the one hand, political and civil liberty, but, on the other, that social and economic inequalities should be to the greatest benefit of the most disadvantaged.[21] This can be a basis for mandating a degree of redistribution or welfare state policies as well as equal opportunities in education and health. Regardless of the view taken of Rawls' particular approach, the implication is that there may be a need to import nonutilitarian political theory into economics if it is desired to justify governments correcting the selfish bias of individual choices and amending the "initial endowment" in the competitive equilibrium, if the equilibrium leaves some citizens vulnerable.

Economics can still give useful policy advice. It is arguably "a useful handmaiden but a bad master." For example, welfare economics tells us that a revised endowment of resources after redistribution could still generate a Pareto-optimal competitive equilibrium. Economics also has an awareness of "market failures," which may necessitate forms of regulation such as those outlined in Appendix 2:

- The first of these market failures is *externality*, where the action of one agent has an unpriced influence on another's welfare. A run on one bank may, for example, lead to runs on others.

- The second is problems arising from *information asymmetry*, such as moral hazard where a set of market prices (or a policy) stimulate individuals to act differently from their underlying needs and preferences to the detriment of the customer or policymaker.

- The third is *monopoly*, which, as noted above, may render a competitive equilibrium impossible to achieve, since monopolists can fix prices at any desired level.

Overall, it can be suggested that economics and its view of humanity offers a good diagnostic analysis of issues in wealth creation and distribution. Application of economic insights to the running of

21. Rawls (1971), 302, uses the theoretical construct of a "veil of ignorance" where individuals choose social arrangements not knowing into which stratum of society they will be born.

economies has provided major benefits in terms of economic development. However, it is weak *normatively* (especially if we do not import "rights" from political theory)—there is a clear focus on efficiency and not on morality.[22] Griffiths argues that economics is often presented (for example by, Friedman, Hayek, and Becker) in a manner that rejects transcendent and absolute moral standards.[23] Indeed, there is typically no awareness of sin or human evil in economics.[24] No prescriptions are made for individual behavior, although economists acknowledge that virtues like trustworthiness and honesty are vital for the smooth running of the economy.[25] Irresponsibility and immoral behavior can only be condemned by economics if they are contrary to individual utility maximization.

Individualism, as is assumed in economics, can naturally be said to promote pride and self-sufficiency. This is the opposite of the Christian view of humanity as appropriately based on relationship with God and with one another, even in its economic behavior. We now turn to a summary of relevant aspects.

2.2 A BIBLICAL VIEW OF HUMANKIND

Like economics, biblical theology looks both at how things *are* (positive) and how things *ought to be* (normative). The Bible focuses strongly on economic aspects of human life and not solely spiritual ones, in line with it being the word of a benevolent creator who cares for all aspects of human life and for the rest of his creation.

Positive Theology

Looking at biblical views of mankind, in a *positive sense*, humanity is seen as being made in the image of God. Mankind has a mandate to order and care for creation, and to obtain from it their food and

---

22. See Griffiths (1984).

23. Griffiths (2001), 30.

24. The overriding assumption that most people act selfishly most of the time might be taken as a fairly robust awareness of sin—albeit without moral criticism implied.

25. See Green (2009), 177.

shelter. This is called the "stewardship mandate" and is introduced in Genesis 1 and 2:

> God blessed them and said to them, "Be fruitful and increase in number; fill the earth and subdue it. Rule over the fish of the sea and the birds of the air and over every living creature that moves on the ground." Then God said, "I give you every seed-bearing plant on the face of the whole earth and every tree that has fruit with seed in it. They will be yours for food."[26] (Genesis 1:28–29)

> The Lord God took the man and put him in the Garden of Eden to work it and take care of it. (Genesis 2:15)

Work is the way in which people carry out their stewardship and express themselves as persons; craftsmen such as Bezalel are celebrated in the Bible and seen as filled with God's Spirit.

> See, I have chosen Bezalel son of Uri, the son of Hur, of the tribe of Judah, and I have filled him with the Spirit of God, with skill, ability, and knowledge in all kinds of crafts—to make artistic designs for work in gold, silver, and bronze, to cut and set stones, to work in wood, and to engage in all kinds of craftsmanship. (Exodus 31:2–5)

This passage, along with others focusing on business and politics —such as the lives of Abraham the pastoral farmer, Joseph the government minister, Jethro the consultant, and Daniel the civil servant—are fully in line with the idea of "secular vocation," promoted by Martin Luther and others. This idea contends that God's call on our lives is not limited to "spiritual" areas of work, such as pastoral ministry and

---

26. The first stewardship mandate is often seen as more aggressive and destructive than the second. This comes notably from the word "subdue" in Genesis 1:28, which is the Hebrew verb *kavash*. Its noun form refers to "a footstool," a place where one places the foot. The verb *kavash* literally implies "to place your foot on the neck of your conquered enemy" signifying a submission of the enemy to his defeater. On the other hand, the word for "rule over" is the Hebrew verb *radah*, which is related to other words that have the meanings of "descend," "go down," "wander," and "spread." This verb literally suggests, "to rule by going down and walking among the subjects as an equal." The use of the two Hebrew verbs *kavash* and *radah* imply that man is to rule over the animals as his subjects, not as a dictator but as a benevolent leader. Man is also to walk among and have a relationship with his subjects so that they can provide for man and that man can "learn" from them (Ancient Hebrew Research Center 2006). There is an obvious link to the way Jesus descended to earth and walked among mankind as an equal.

mission work. Rather, *any* morally acceptable area of work can be a kingdom vocation—including work in the financial services sector.

Meanwhile, like God, humans are personal beings, able to make choices, and also able to come into relationship with other living beings. Griffiths notes that "the creator is revealed to us as a rational, moral, feeling person capable of making choices, and God's image in man implies that he is [the same]."[27]

But mankind is also *fallen*, having disobeyed God in Eden. As such, choices and actions can be determined by self-interest, relationships can be spoiled by power and fear, humanity may exploit nature rather than care for it, and work can become toil, as foreshadowed in the "curse of Eden":

> To Adam he said, "Because you listened to your wife and ate from the tree about which I commanded you, 'You must not eat of it,' cursed is the ground because of you; through painful toil you will eat of it all the days of your life. It will produce thorns and thistles for you, and you will eat the plants of the field. By the sweat of your brow you will eat your food until you return to the ground, since from it you were taken; for dust you are and to dust you will return." (Genesis 3:17–19)

People are frequently shown in the Bible to "do as they see fit" (Judges 21:25), generally following their own selfish interests.

Accordingly, there is a mixture in what we observe of human behavior, including in the economic field, of the holy and the fallen. The economic analysis described above is perhaps an approximation or parallel to fallen, self-interested behavior under the curse of Eden. Work is seen as a disutility, actions are directed to maximize personal utility on a selfish basis, while mediation of transactions via impersonal markets may allow us to ignore power relations between individuals. But the economic approach can still be criticized for ignoring the reality of power relations and negative spiritual influences that theology acknowledges. Furthermore, there are also still aspects of the holy in human behavior, such as altruism. Biblical theology states that people should be seen as ends valued by God for themselves, and not just as means to ends (i.e., to productive work, to utility generation), as is often the case in the worldview of economics. Work is widely valued

27. Griffiths (1980).

in itself or as a part of human dignity, not simply as "disutility." In Scripture, relationships may be affected by commitment and not just by personal utility. The degree to which the fallen and holy relate will depend on individuals but also on culture.

Theology, unlike economics, takes note of structural aspects that may overlay individual behavior, such as the unjust laws criticized in Isaiah 10:1–2:

> Woe to those who make unjust laws, to those who issue oppressive decrees, to deprive the poor of their rights and withhold justice from the oppressed of my people, making widows their prey and robbing the fatherless.

Structural sin is a particular focus of "liberation theologians,"[28] who link it to violation of human rights, disempowerment of the poor, and also economic injustice, "favoring greed [of the rich] at the expense of the life and dignity [of the poor]."[29] Such structural sin may be manifest in the market economy itself. The "sin of the world" (John 1:29) makes it hard for those who benefit to discern systemic evil and its sources. Liberation theology argues that the Bible encourages Christians to oppose "structural injustice" in politics and economics for it leads to poverty, which in turn reflects the influence of the devil on "the world" as, for example, in Ephesians 2:1–2:

> As for you, you were dead in your transgressions and sins, in which you used to live when you followed the ways of this world and of the ruler of the kingdom of the air, the spirit who is now at work in those who are disobedient.

Liberation theologians argue that owing to the imbalance of power and influence, markets themselves may be vulnerable to binding and oppressing the poor, a situation from which markets need to be redeemed.

On the other hand, the Bible does not assert that markets *per se* are a negative thing. Throughout the Bible, individuals specialize and produce, buy and sell products for their wider needs, as in the modern economy, be it by barter or cash transactions, as well as in subsistence. The early liberation theologians arguably based too much of

28. White and Tiongco (1997), 64.
29. Fitzgerald, (1999), 224.

their analysis of society on an uncritical borrowing from a broadly Marxist economics (indeed, this was the thrust of the Vatican's condemnation of liberation theology, issued in 1984), and so offered an overly negative view of markets.

The view of humanity from theology is more rounded and complete than that of economics. As already noted, community life is crucial to our humanity—not just individual fulfillment or the impersonality of transactions in a market. Indeed, Israel—and later Jesus himself—are seen as representative of humanity and thus able to stand before God on behalf of the rest of humanity, a group identification that goes well beyond the individualism of economics. Christians are called to be together in community as the church. God repeatedly speaks to *nations* and *groups*, not merely to individuals. *Humanity is essentially relational*: Adam is incomplete without Eve; all human beings need a relation with God himself. Indeed, the doctrine of the Trinity teaches us that *God is relational*, so human beings, made in his image, are inevitably relational also. Accordingly, emotions such as love and hatred, which are interpersonal, are of relevance to behavior. As noted by Britton and Sedgwick, "economics cannot comprehend *love* because of its prior commitment to rational calculation, but also because of its prior commitment to individualism."[30] Economics cannot give any account of *trust*, either, which is a paradox since trust between people is essential to the efficient working of markets.

Although the Bible sometimes celebrates wealth as a blessing from God, and goods we consume are seen as coming from the benevolent creator, it is the relationship with God that a Christian sees as central to well-being. Indeed, Jesus states firmly that we are blessed if we are poor (Luke 6:20) or identify with the poor. Riches can blind us to the needs of others and the need for a relationship with God.

Paul sees church at its best as a loving fellowship, willing to share with the needy among them, being generous to imitate the overwhelming generosity of Christ himself:

> For you know the grace of our Lord Jesus Christ, that though he was rich, yet for your sakes he became poor, so that you through his poverty might become rich. (2 Corinthians 8:9)

30. Britton and Sedgwick (2003), 246.

When Paul meets Peter and the other apostles in Jerusalem, they are agreed that "remembering the poor" should be at the heart of the life of the churches that Paul will plant (Galatians 2:10). Wealth is a responsibility, something we must steward for the benefit of others, even as mankind is called to steward creation itself. A corollary is seeing work as a form of service to bless others. Beyond that, well-being incorporates the promise of eternal life with Christ, ultimately in the new heaven and the new earth. All these kingdom benefits are not to be gained by selfishly maximizing but by accepting Jesus as our Savior and Lord, and showing love to all. The core of Christianity is not about "doing good" (that could be integrated in economics via a suitable utility function), it is to do with a relationship with God himself, and love for others, which stems from gratitude for his generosity to us:

> For it is by grace you have been saved, through faith—and this not from yourselves, it is the gift of God—not by works, so that no one can boast. For we are God's workmanship, created in Christ Jesus to do good works, which God prepared in advance for us to do. (Ephesians 2:8–10)

Note that there is a strand of the evangelical tradition that does stress self-interest as the key motivation of humanity, but self-interest is redefined in the light of the gospel. The promise of heavenly joys for all eternity is so much a better *good* than anything else we can aspire to, that to ignore every other desire and hope in order to focus on gaining heaven is a rational decision.

Consequently, the most important choice does not relate to consumption, saving, or labor supply, Rather, it is the choice of salvation itself, entailing repentance from sins. Openness to God's love and fulfilling the destiny he has given is the essence of humanity. Fulfillment is found in serving God, not in going our own way. In a wider context of spiritual reality, it must be clarified that the issue of "rational choice" is not about weighing preferences but instead about attempting to embody a particular style of life, following Jesus. The choice to follow him is true freedom in relationship, in the same way as the Trinity is in eternal loving relationship. This freedom is, of course, contrary to the popular view that becoming a Christian involves a sacrifice of freedom.

Normative Theology

Normatively, the Bible suggests an ethical focus to the theological view of mankind, with *justice* as a core. There is less fear of value judgments and "blaming" than one finds in economics. Both individual behaviors and social situations are subject to critique. For, being made in the image of God, man has free choice, but also he is responsible morally for the choices he makes. The Bible emphasizes the risk that money becomes an idol, and the economic system gives rise to a form of structural injustice—although theology also highlights the need for private property under God to protect against poverty.

In the light of Christ's sacrifice on the cross, Christians are called to be "redeemers of fallen creation" in advance of the new heaven and new earth:

> The creation waits in eager expectation for the sons of God to be revealed. For the creation was subjected to frustration, not by its own choice, but by the will of the one who subjected it, in hope that the creation itself will be liberated from its bondage to decay and brought into the glorious freedom of the children of God. (Romans 8:19–21)

This implies being stewards of resources in the way God intended —suggesting that it is essential for Christians to focus on current economic issues. Godly stewards are wise, generous, and trustworthy, recognizing that it is *God's* resources we deal with in our economic lives. In this world, money is a necessary resource for almost everything we try to do, so it can be argued that a pious refusal to be interested in economics in the way it affects us all amounts to a refusal of our Christian duty.

A Christian critique of the normative approach of economics could include, first, the idea of "the good."[31] A Christian approach would go much wider than the economic view of maximizing personal satisfaction in pursuit of individual preferences, usually understood in terms of hedonism. Jesus taught us to love God and our neighbor,[32] stretching the notion of love much wider than the individual and his family.[33] Second, Christian ethicists broadly agree that morality is

31. See Hay (1989), 58–89.

32. The Good Samaritan of Luke 10:25–37 illustrates this point well.

33. John Piper's (1986) account of "Christian hedonism" is based on the belief

about actions and not merely consequences. God's law spells out what he requires of mankind in daily life, such as righteous <u>motives</u> (not purely for self-aggrandizement at the expense of others), righteous actions (e.g., not lying), maintenance of social institutions that God has ordained (such as marriage and the sanctity of human life), and sensitivity to justice (as in global poverty). As the prophet Micah says:

> He has showed you, O man, what is good. And what does the Lord require of you? To act justly and to love mercy and to walk humbly with your God. (Micah 6:8)

So, concern by the economist for efficiency, growth, and (in some cases) equality, is replaced, or at least supplemented, by a concern for stewardship, useful work, protection of the vulnerable, and the preservation of <u>marriage and family life.</u>

Furthermore, a Christian would see a benefit to community itself, going beyond simple aggregation of individuals. Rather, <u>community</u> <u>can be seen as good in itself</u>, both for the individual concerned as well as for others because it makes it easier to fulfill the duty to help one's neighbor. So the goals of the individual should be related to those of the community and not be solely individualistic. The value given to community is based not only on the way God designed humanity (Genesis 2:18, where God states "it is not good for man to be alone") but also the fact that God himself is a relational being as Father, Son, and Holy Spirit.

A Christian view of the state differs from an economic view. As noted, some economists see the state as a threat to economic outcomes that would be best served by laissez-faire. Others economists, as a theoretical construct, might see the state as needing only a benevolent dictator imposing what in their view is the optimal allocation of resources on a reluctant society. A Christian view is that the state is ordained by God to keep the peace and administer justice, preventing evil that would arise from anarchy, as Paul writes in the book of Romans:

> Everyone must submit himself to the governing authorities, for there is no authority except that which God has established. The authorities that exist have been established by God. Consequently, he who rebels against the authority is rebelling

---

that we find true happiness precisely in loving God and neighbor, and so Christian living is the way to authentic self-fulfillment.

against what God has instituted, and those who do so will bring judgment on themselves. For rulers hold no terror for those who do right, but for those who do wrong. Do you want to be free from fear of the one in authority? Then do what is right and he will commend you. For he is God's servant to do you good. But if you do wrong, be afraid, for he does not bear the sword for nothing. He is God's servant, an agent of wrath to bring punishment on the wrongdoer. Therefore, it is necessary to submit to the authorities, not only because of possible punishment but also because of conscience. This is also why you pay taxes, for the authorities are God's servants, who give their full time to governing. Give everyone what you owe him: If you owe taxes, pay taxes; if revenue, then revenue; if respect, then respect; if honor, then honor. (Romans 13:1–7)

A realistic view is taken of the fall, and hence the need for enforcement of order. There is a duty to obey the state, but equally rulers are seen as under God, and hence responsible to him; the state's decisions should still be monitored critically from a biblical standpoint. However, Christians would stand alongside most economists in opposing a dictatorial state threatening freedom. And it is notable that regimes that seek to suppress markets have often been those that deny human rights, including free exercise of religious faith.[34]

To summarize this chapter, we note the following eight suggestions by Hay for extensions of the economic "good" beyond consumption, leisure, and economic efficiency if a Christian viewpoint is adopted.[35] These focus on responsibilities as well as rights, with the key word being stewardship:[36]

First, humanity must use the resources of creation to provide for themselves, but not destroy the created order (as in the stewardship mandate of Genesis 1:28–29). God's creation is good and we can enjoy consuming its fruits in moderation.

Second, each person has a calling to exercise stewardship of talents and resources, as in the Parable of the Talents:

The man who had received the five talents brought the other five. "Master," he said, "you entrusted me with five talents. See, I have gained five more." His master replied, "Well done, good

34. Griffiths (2001), 29.
35. Hay (1989), 72–77.
36. See also Smith (2005).

> and faithful servant! You have been faithful with a few things;
> I will put you in charge of many things. Come and share your
> master's happiness!" (Matthew 25:20–21)

Third, stewardship implies a responsibility to determine the disposition of resources. Each person is accountable to God for his stewardship. As in Psalm 24:1–2, the land ultimately belongs to *God*, not the private owner.

> The earth is the Lord's, and everything in it, the world, and all
> who live in it; for he founded it upon the seas and established
> it upon the waters.

Fourth, people have a right and an obligation to work, as in Eden where Adam is set to work it and take care of it (Genesis 2:15).

Fifth, work is a means of exercising stewardship. In work, human beings should have access to and control over fairly distributed resources, as is ensured, for example, by provisions in the Jubilee for land to always return to the family in Leviticus:

> Throughout the country that you hold as a possession, you
> must provide for the redemption of the land. If one of your
> countrymen becomes poor and sells some of his property, his
> nearest relative is to come and redeem what his countryman has
> sold. If, however, a man has no one to redeem it for him but he
> himself prospers and acquires sufficient means to redeem it, he
> is to determine the value for the years since he sold it and re-
> fund the balance to the man to whom he sold it; he can then go
> back to his own property. But if he does not acquire the means
> to repay him, what he sold will remain in the possession of the
> buyer until the Year of Jubilee. It will be returned in the Jubilee,
> and he can then go back to his property. (Leviticus 25:24–28)

Sixth, work is a social activity in which people cooperate as stewards of their individual talents and as joint stewards of resources, as in the church considered as a body to which all contribute:

> The body is a unit, though it is made up of many parts; and
> though all its parts are many, they form one body. So it is with
> Christ. For we were all baptized by one Spirit into one body—
> whether Jews or Greeks, slave or free—and we were all given the
> one Spirit to drink. Now the body is not made up of one part but
> of many. (1 Corinthians 12:12–14)

Seventh, each person has a right to share in God's provision for humankind, for basic needs of food, clothing, and shelter, and these should be provided by productive work, as seen in provision for the poor to share in the harvest:

> When you are harvesting in your field and you overlook a sheaf, do not go back to get it. Leave it for the alien, the fatherless and the widow, so that the Lord your God may bless you in all the work of your hands. When you beat the olives from your trees, do not go over the branches a second time. Leave what remains for the alien, the fatherless and the widow. When you harvest the grapes in your vineyard, do not go over the vines again. Leave what remains for the alien, the fatherless and the widow. Remember that you were slaves in Egypt. That is why I command you to do this. (Deuteronomy 24:19–22)

gleaning

And eighth, personal stewardship of resources does not imply the right to consume the entire product of those resources. The rich have an obligation to help the poor who cannot provide for themselves by work, as Jesus emphasizes in the rich man and Lazarus, for example:

> There was a rich man who was dressed in purple and fine linen and lived in luxury every day. At his gate was laid a beggar named Lazarus, covered with sores and longing to eat what fell from the rich man's table. Even the dogs came and licked his sores. The time came when the beggar died and the angels carried him to Abraham's side. The rich man also died and was buried. In hell, where he was in torment, he looked up and saw Abraham far away, with Lazarus by his side. (Luke 16:19–23)

Considering this chapter as a whole, we do not deny that economics and the market-based economy and financial system have provided huge benefits in terms of wealth generation that have assisted the whole of society. But from a Christian perspective, there remains an unease with the lack of moral foundations for economics, as taught to millions, at its most basic level.

There are two aspects, first amorality *per se*, and, second, a reduced view of what it is to be human (with no account of relationships, for instance). These points mean that economics needs to be supplemented, at the very least, by values from humanistic political theory, but better by enlightened understanding offered by Scripture.

With this comparison and contrast as background, we now turn to an examination of the teachings of economics and theology relevant to three key elements of the financial crisis: first, the behavior of bankers; second, the rise in household debt; and, third, the explosion of public debt. By confronting in each case the distinctive approaches of economics and theology, we seek to develop a kingdom view of personal behavior and policy recommendations.

Chapter 3

The Financial Sector—Incentives to Underestimate Risks

3.1 FROM AN ECONOMICS PERSPECTIVE

Given the central role of banks and bankers in the crisis, as outlined in chapter 1 above, we focus first on issues in banking. What could have led to the catastrophic underestimation of risks that preceded the crisis? The economic role of financial institutions such as banks in the modern economy is a crucial one. Merton and Bodie suggest that it can be summarized in six functions of the financial system.[1] These are:

- The provision of means for clearing and settling payments to facilitate exchange of goods, services, and assets. An example is check clearing and other forms of payment for goods and services that banks provide.

- The provision of a mechanism for pooling funds from individual households so as to facilitate large-scale indivisible undertakings like firms or construction projects, and the subdivision of shares in enterprises to facilitate diversification. So, for example, bank deposits are pooled to make loans to mortgage holders, while banks are enterprises issuing shares for growth of their business.

1. Merton and Bodie (1995).

- The provision of means to transfer economic resources over time, across geographic regions, countries, or industries. Bank loans enable short-term savings to be transformed into long-term lending that can take place cross-border as well as to different places within a country.

- The provision of means to manage uncertainty and control risk. Banks seek to carry out "due diligence" credit analysis in lending to ensure that the borrower has the capacity to repay loans.

- Providing price information, thus helping to coordinate decentralized decision making in various sectors of the economy. This is the function of the stock and bond markets, which set prices for financial assets but in which banks are highly active.

- Providing means to deal with incentive problems when one party to a financial transaction has information the other does not, or when one is an agent of the other, and when control and enforcement of contracts is costly. So banks devise contracts that seek to provide incentives for loans to be repaid, overcoming the difficulties that economists call adverse selection and moral hazard. An example of adverse selection in banking is a tendency for banks that seek to grow rapidly to get lots of bad credits, since they are lending to the borrowers other banks have rejected. An example of moral hazard in banking is a tendency of borrowers who are not monitored properly by the bank to misuse the money they are lent.

A first remark is that it is self-evident that widespread bank failure, threatening provision of these functions, is extremely damaging to the economy. This explains both the amplitude of the downturn and also the efforts by governments to support banks, as discussed in chapter 1 above.

A second remark is that the performance of these functions requires integrity and prudence on the part of bankers in performing their functions—as was repeatedly, perhaps routinely, lacking in many institutions in recent years. Notably, financial institutions need to avoid the temptation to provide credit too readily to individuals, firms, and governments in a way that entails excessive risk to their institution. Once underpriced loans had been made, banks were vulnerable to the consequences of default, directly and via securitized claims, when borrowers' financial situations worsened. Equally they need to ensure their institutions have access to reliable sources of liquidity, to avoid the risk of "runs."[2] And furthermore, they need to ensure their institutions have adequate capital and provisions to cover unexpected and expected losses (see Appendix 2). Failure to carry out such "due diligence"—as was the case in the sub-prime crisis, as described in chapter 1—threatens the economy as a whole and not just the bank concerned, if it is sufficiently widespread.

In this context, a dangerous pattern may have been created by a combination of the bonus culture of banks and the "safety net" provided by the government. Bonus schemes in banks, which may account for as much as 50 percent of remuneration, often reward the short-term performance of an individual trader or lending officer. This, in turn, can lead them to focus on raising short-term returns, with no attention paid to the risk of greater losses in the future. Means of obtaining high returns would include, first, lending large volumes at high risk, say to sub-prime borrowers or buy-to-let investors (with high interest rates and also fees attached), without concern for long-term risk. Second, it would include purchase of large volumes of high yielding securities (such as sub-prime ABS) without taking a view of their long-term valuation.

Behavior of chief executives and other board members may also have been influenced by performance incentives such as stock option plans and stock bonuses. These incentives may, in turn, have caused costly strategic errors by managers. These errors include seeking growth of the institution beyond what was feasible with retail deposits via use of risky wholesale deposits; and allowing capital and liquid asset cover to be reduced and thus boosting profitability at a cost of enhanced risk of insolvency (see Appendix 2). It also entailed aggressive takeovers of other banks at the peak of the boom when share prices were very high, financed by debt. This left some of the buying institutions (such as RBS and Lehmans) highly vulnerable to failure.

The background to this pattern of behavior, notably for the strategic decisions of chief executives, was knowledge that the authorities simply could not let major banks fail, and would have to support

2. See also the discussion in Appendix 2.

them initially via "lender of last resort" liquidity support and later via recapitalization and guarantees at taxpayers' expense. The bankers, in effect, had an incentive to underprice risk, partly because of asymmetric payoffs—the profits would accrue in bonuses and option revaluation, the losses, in the end, to the taxpayers if the bank is "too big to fail" and so is supported by the central bank and government. This is another form of moral hazard, the outcome of a guarantee that generates risky behavior (by bankers), which is adverse to the provider of that guarantee (the state).

Note that these incentives are not so favorable for shareholders, who may lose out in a government "rescue." Indeed, pension funds of individual employees lost out greatly owing to the devaluation of banking shares. The shareholder's voice in a limited liability company such as a bank is not a strong one, even for major institutional investors, except in the case of major failures of "corporate governance."[3] This is partly due to lack of sufficiently detailed information on the firm, as well as lack of sanctions apart from selling to a takeover raider. An additional issue for portfolio index funds that sell themselves on low fees is the desire to minimize costs of intervention. Shareholders were accordingly unable or unwilling to restrain the rush for profitability by taking high levels of risk that banks undertook in the period up to 2007.

Such an explanation of banker's behavior as that set out above suggests direct culpability, with actions taken in full knowledge of the related risks. This is consistent with the economic model of humanity as pursuing self-interest. There may also be indirect channels of causality. Notably, there may have been "disaster myopia," whereby lenders forgot there could be bad times again. In other words, it is possible that lack of insight was a part of the problem, as well as a lack of integrity or prudence. As in the run-up to past crises, people start to believe "it's different this time"[4] (e.g., due to the fact that claims were securitized). They forget the lessons of the past, namely that a credit and asset price boom often ends in a financial crisis, as for example in the US and UK in 1989–91.[5] This pattern of individual and institutional

3. Davis and Steil (2001), ch. 6.

4. See Reinhart and Rogoff (2010) for an account of financial crises proving the folly of believing that "this times it's different."

5. See Appendix 1 and Reinhart and Rogoff (2010).

forgetfulness may be provoked by the same asymmetry of outcomes for employees/managers and the state/shareholders, making bankers focus on the short-term only. But it <u>is clearly contrary to the main-stream economic assumption of "rationality."</u>   I disagree - it was Rational due to asymmetry

Historically, banks have often been vulnerable to patterns of loss-es from loans held on the balance sheet (e.g., in the 1973 crisis of the UK secondary banks; the Latin American debt crisis of 1982; the US Savings and Loans crises of 1979–89; and the Japanese, Swedish, and Finnish banking crises that began in 1991).[6] However, it can be argued that the securitized products such as ABS that abounded in the run-up to the crisis were particularly vulnerable to abuse in terms of under-playing of risk and/or disaster myopia. As innovations, the behavior of ABS under stress was not yet known—like a new drug whose full range of side effects has not been tested.

Also there are a wide range of "information gaps" in ABS where those taking decisions did not bear the consequences of poor out-comes, while those who did suffer the consequences did not under-stand the risk, due to complexity and poor information. For example, those banks making sub-prime loans in the US would sell them as bonds, so passing the risk to others who lacked detailed information on the loans involved. They had much less reason to worry about credit quality than if they held the loans on their books. Furthermore, the "rating agencies" that are supposed to make independent assess-ments of credit risk actually made excessively optimistic assessments of such risk for these instruments, no doubt partly following their own self-interest in generating fees from the issuers.

The overall situation was worsened by the "<u>principal-agent prob-lem</u>," which is endemic in banking. The "principal" owns the assets but gets someone else, his "agent," to look after them. For example, the shareholders of a bank like Lehmans or RBS (the principal) man-date the managers of the bank to be the agent and run the company on their behalf. But the problem is that the agent may easily act in his or her own interest and not that of the owner, if they are not trust-worthy, being driven by greed. Richard Fuld of Lehmans and Sir Fred Goodwin of RBS made disastrous overpriced takeovers that contrib-uted to the ruin of their banks. It would appear that money managers

---

6. For a description of the events of these crises see Davis (1995), chs. 6 and 8.

like Bernard Madoff and Allen Stanford directly defrauded people who had entrusted money to them.

There are three ways in economics to deal with principal-agent problems, which is, in effect, the way the subject deals with a key part of business ethics. It is assumed that a self-interested person will behave ethically if there are sufficient incentives.

The first resolution of the principal-agent problem is to draw up a "complete contract" that specifies the agent's behavior in every circumstance, or at least seeks to align perfectly the interests of the agent and principal. But this is generally seen as impossible, as witness the difficulty banks have had with annual bonuses. While bonuses are assumed to give rise to appropriate incentives to maximize profits for the institution, they actually led to risk taking by employees that wrecked some institutions.

A second resolution is to rely on reputation. If the agent sees their reputation for honesty as an asset, they will be trustworthy because it's in their own interests. People can, after all, be fired, and institutions can fail or be taken over. Spoil your reputation once and no one will trust you again—at least for a few years. But this is more effective for a single individual or institution that behaves differently from the rest. In the credit boom, bankers were comforted by the fact that all their counterparts were acting in the same way, and hence, except for the most egregious cases, the risk to reputation from risk taking was small.

And the third resolution is ongoing relationships. In economics, people are supposed to act in a trustworthy manner in an ongoing relationship, such as an employment relationship or a link with a client, so as to keep the benefits of that relationship, which would otherwise be spoiled. But economics sees mankind as totally selfish, so the relationship will be abandoned if the person considers it to be in their interest. We noted earlier that the idea of commitment (loyalty, love) is absent from the bulk of economic analysis. Furthermore, the form of banking that developed in the 2000s, with loans being securitized and sold piecewise to investors round the world, is inimical to the form of banking relationships typical of traditional banking, where managers would know their own clients and deal with them on a regular basis. So again the sanction was weak.

We have seen that protection from deposit insurance and the lender of last resort (the government "safety net") offers banks[7] an incentive to take risks. For this reason, economics stresses a need for prudential regulation as a form of protection for the "safety net," as well as for depositors, against banks' risk taking (see Appendix 2).[8] Banks must be obliged to hold sufficient capital, while liquidity should also be held in spite of the bankers' incentives to minimize it. There might also be supervision of the incentive schemes in banks.

But in fact it would appear that the authorities had allowed liquidity regulation to be excessively lax; the bonus culture was rarely investigated and capital adequacy was not maintained with sufficient rigor. It can be suggested that the regulators, too, were subject to "disaster myopia,"[9] perhaps influenced in part by fear of loss of national competitive position if their regulations were tighter than elsewhere. They also failed to see the presence of difficulties at a system-wide level, as opposed to within individual institutions. Hence the calls at present for much tighter regulation, notably of the bonus culture and of banks' capital as well as at a system-wide or "macroprudential" level.[10]

To sum up, while economics offers an understanding on the importance of banks and the incentives and motivations for bankers' behavior, there remain puzzles from the point of view of the "rational economic humanity" paradigm. For example, why is there the irrationality implicit in "disaster myopia," which is a huge departure from the paradigms discussed in chapter 2? Why did firms invest massively in securities whose properties they did not understand? Why were takeovers undertaken at excessive prices, which threatened the bidding firm's solvency? Equally, economics is silent on the issues of

7. Although technically only commercial banks should benefit from it, in practice US investment banks also benefited from "safety net" protection, with the exception of Lehmans.

8. There are various regulations on loans (such as on "large exposures") to prevent the bank becoming insufficiently diversified and thus increasing the risk of insolvency. Prudential regulation also focuses on management and earnings as important to risk management and ability to grow capital, respectively. Overarching these may be "structural regulations" that limit competition between banks and, hence, limit the degree of risk on the asset side (since competition typically induces banks to seek higher returns at higher risk).

9. See Davis (2008, 2009).

10. See Basel Committee (2011).

prudence, trust, and honesty that are essential to the functioning of financial markets in the long term. We now turn to a Christian view to see what additional insights are available.

3.2 FROM A THEOLOGICAL PERSPECTIVE

While the sophistication of the modern financial system is absent from Scripture, the underlying ethical issues are not, including those related directly to business ethics. Indeed, they are apparent already in the fall story of Genesis.[11]

A first aspect was that of hubris, as set out in Genesis 3. Adam and Eve were tempted by the serpent to eat the fruit of the tree of knowledge. The serpent said to Eve:

> for God knows that when you eat of it your eyes will be opened,
> and you will be like God, knowing good and evil. (Genesis 3:5)

And they found this temptation irresistible. In business, there can be corruption arising from the desire for power and success, leading to arrogant behavior, which can entail disaster myopia with risk taking at the individual level (such as excessive purchase of risky securities) or the firm's strategic level (such as inappropriate takeovers). In business, previous success can feed such attitudes, with a false and hubristic sense of invulnerability leading to serious risks being ignored. Pride leads individuals to overlook risks, as well as to seek financial gain.

Similarly, the account of Babel in Genesis 11 describes individuals seeking to be like God, building empires for their own glory like the bank conglomerates built during the boom:

> Then they said, "Come, let us build ourselves a city, with a tower that reaches to the heavens, so that we may make a name for ourselves and not be scattered over the face of the whole earth."
> (Genesis 11:4)

The expressed desire in that verse is "to make a name for ourselves," clearly a prideful attitude. James 4 speaks of individuals boasting about the future profits they would make.

> Now listen, you who say, "Today or tomorrow we will go to this or that city, spend a year there, carry on business, and make

11. Higginson (1993), 83–89.

money." Why, you do not even know what will happen tomorrow. What is your life? You are a mist that appears for a little while and then vanishes. Instead, you ought to say, "If it is the Lord's will, we will live and do this or that." (James 4:13–15)

Desire to make a name for themselves and the paradoxical underlying insecurity it betrays may underlie the dominance of banks by empire builders such as Dick Fuld of Lehmans, who overreached themselves and brought down their institutions. They reportedly refused to hear news contrary to their own views. We saw above that desire to protect reputation is one protection against principal-agent problems, but Scripture shows its limitations. There is a realism about human psychology in the Bible that economic theory needs to take more seriously.

A further issue in the Eden story relevant to banking crises is the breakdown of the relationship of cooperation between human beings that came with the fall, entailing the abusive use of power and exploitation. The specific example is that of men and women, where God says to Eve:

"Your desire will be for your husband, and he will rule over you."
(Genesis 3:16)

There is a clear link from such corruption in human relationships to banking ethics, where competition rather than cooperation within firms helped build up risk—traders competed with one another to maximize their profits and hence their bonuses. Equally, leadership in firms, which should be benign and for the benefit of all, can become dictatorial, as at Lehmans, in the same way that marital relationships can sour. We saw above that ongoing quality of relationships is one protection against principal-agent problems, but Scripture again shows its limitations.

There can also be the "blame game":

The man said, "The woman you put here with me—she gave me some fruit from the tree, and I ate it." Then the Lord God said to the woman, "What is this you have done?" The woman said, "The serpent deceived me, and I ate." (Genesis 3:12–13)

Here Adam and Eve accuse one another and the serpent of being the guilty party—and Adam implicitly also blames God ("the woman you gave me"). People in business often seek to avoid responsibility, because of its effect on future reputation and employment, although that is dishonest. And when no one is willing to take responsibility for a firm's actions, then the outcome may well be adverse, as many firms found out in the banking crisis.

Turning to wider biblical witness relevant to bankers' behavior, there is the issue of the quality of their work, which may also underlie their risky actions. With the fall there is a curse on work (Genesis 3:17–19 quoted on page 23 above), while Ecclesiastes says:

> What does a man get for all the toil and anxious striving with which he labors under the sun? All his days his work is pain and grief; even at night his mind does not rest. (Ecclesiastes 2:22–23)

This could certainly apply to overstressed bankers and may help explain why they were willing to put their jobs at risk for pecuniary reward, if the work itself was seen as unrewarding.

Furthermore the Bible is replete with examples of irrational behavior, such as the Israelites worshipping gods who are mere blocks of wood (Isaiah 44:12–20) as summarized by Isaiah:

> They know nothing, they understand nothing; their eyes are plastered over so they cannot see, and their minds closed so they cannot understand. (Isaiah 44:18)

Hence irrational and idolatrous[12] behavior for bankers is hardly a surprise. A more explicit example of myopia is shown in Isaiah 56:

> "Come," each one cries, "let me get wine! Let us drink our fill of beer! And tomorrow will be like today, or even far better." (Isaiah 56:12)

No precautionary provision for hard times, in other words. Again, this time in humorous ways, the biblical picture of human character and motivation shows a realism about our frequent irrationality that seems missing from some economic analysis.

Despite the fall, there remains a biblical value placed on quality of work, the concept of "secular vocation," which Green contends sketches out a positive framework that bankers and others should

---

12. In the sense of pursuing financial gain for its own sake, as a type of god.

follow.[13] This is evident, for example, in the skilled work of Bezalel on the tabernacle, which is celebrated in Exodus 31:2–5 (quoted above), and which was accompanied by his being "filled with the Spirit of God." This work was not just for the self; he also taught others:

> [God] has given both him [Bezalel] and Oholiab son of Ahisamach, of the tribe of Dan, the ability to teach others. (Exodus 35:34)

In Proverbs the skilled man is praised because "he will serve before kings; he will not serve before obscure men" (Proverbs 22:29).

Jesus' Parable of the Talents (Matthew 25:14–30 cited on page 29 above) encourages hard work in the context of the skills God has given us, while Luke 10:7 says that "the worker deserves his wages." This implies that it is not wrong biblically for bankers, or any other employees, to strive for better salaries and promotion. On the other hand, Paul says in Colossians that we should

> work with all our heart, as working for the Lord and not for men. (Colossians 3:23)

In other words, we should not focus solely on "impressing the boss" for promotion or a bonus, but work hard for God's honor.

Karl Barth suggests that we are called to be servants of God and our fellow human beings;[14] our work in this light then entails sustaining and directing the world, and seeking the welfare of creation. Consistent with this, Griffiths argues that work generally, and market enterprise more specifically, can be seen to have a legitimacy based on the "creation mandate" to order creation for mankind's needs.[15] Furthermore, drawing on Martin Luther's concept of the goodness of all human vocations, Weber produced the well-known sociological analysis of the significance of the "Protestant work ethic."[16] Weber's analysis suggests that these biblical ideas have informed Western models of work and leisure, and our ethics of employment, to a significant extent. For example, the idea that work provides human beings with meaning and significance is clearly in line with biblical teaching.

13. Green (1988), 106–19.
14. Barth (1960).
15. Griffiths (2001), 23.
16. Weber (2002).

Whereas the texts quoted above encourage hard work, which was certainly evident in Wall Street and the City, the Bible also enjoins integrity. Virtues such as honesty are stressed by the Ten Commandments and in Leviticus 19:11–12. Indeed, many of the commands—such as "do not lie," "do not deceive one another," "do not swear falsely by my name and so profane the name of your God," and "do not defraud your neighbor or rob him"—relate to honesty. Another key kingdom virtue relevant to our work lives is putting others' interests before one's own. Paul offers the command:

> Do nothing out of selfish ambition or vain conceit, but in humility consider others better than yourselves. Each of you should look not only to your own interests, but also to the interests of others. (Philippians 2:3–4)

before memorably citing the example of Christ:

> Who, being in very nature God, did not consider equality with God something to be grasped, but made himself nothing, taking the very nature of a servant, being made in human likeness. And being found in appearance as a man, he humbled himself and became obedient to death—even death on a cross! (Philippians 2:6–8)

Both honesty and selflessness were absent in many firms in the banking crisis, as shown in chapter 1 above. A word often used for hard work in the Bible is "diligence," as in the rebuilding of Jerusalem's walls in Ezra 5:8. This has a deeper meaning in banking—"due diligence" means assessing correctly all the risks before undertaking a transaction, a virtue sadly lacking in the run-up to 2007. The fact that it was possible to avoid such difficulties is evident from the fact that some institutions either avoided investing in "toxic debt" entirely or withdrew when market conditions began to worsen.

Turning more specifically to biblical material relevant to banking, diversification of portfolios is comparable to Solomon's recommendation to hedge risk of disaster:

> Cast your bread upon the waters, for after many days you will find it again. Give portions to seven, yes to eight, for you do not know what disaster may come upon the land. (Ecclesiastes 11:1–2)

It was evident that sub-prime ABS did not diversify sufficiently the underlying credit risk, in the way securitized products are supposed to. In the light of this, banks became vulnerable to liquidity and credit risk when the assets underlying the ABS defaulted and liquidity in the ABS collapsed. And although on the liability side banks may have used a variety of wholesale funding sources and instruments, they did not allow sufficiently for a complete collapse of the wholesale funding market.

The Bible's warnings about false weights and measures used to deceive customers could be seen as linked to the inaccurate ratings of the credit rating agencies for the structured products.

> The Lord detests differing weights, and dishonest scales do not please him. (Proverbs 20:23)

These inaccuracies were apparently encouraged by the financial rewards from giving easy ratings to such products as well as resulting from mistakes due to inaccurate models and intense competition between the agencies.[17] The falsification can also be seen as contrary to the second commandment, to treat others as we would like to be treated ourselves.

We will discuss in chapter 4 below the controversy regarding interest and usury, which has implications for banks. Suffice to note here that traditional Christian teaching regarded all lending (except that freely undertaken at zero interest) with suspicion. Calvin said that under the "law of love" and good stewardship, there could be no objection to loans on reasonable terms between equal parties with good business reasons to lend and borrow, hence legitimizing banking.[18] But the law of love and stewardship that Calvin advocates would not permit many of the unjust and exploitative practices undertaken in the boom. These included lending to often poorly educated and low-income sub-prime

17. The models of the rating agencies failed to take into account the possibility that US house prices could fall nationally as well as regionally, because it had rarely happened in the past. Furthermore, there were some specific coding errors in the models that came to light before the crisis took place.

18. As noted by Graafland (2009), 3, Calvin argued that "the productivity of labour is greatly enhanced if it is combined with capital. With the investment loan, the debtor is able to obtain additional income. A trader can, for instance, gain a great amount of money with someone else's money. Hence, it is fair that the lender is compensated. Rewarding the supplier of capital is therefore as natural and fair as paying rent for the use of land or a house."

borrowers without adequate warning of the risk of homelessness, and without sufficient explanation of the sharp future rises in interest rates once initial low "teaser" interest rates finished.[19]

An important clue to Jesus' view of the appropriate conduct of the trade of finance is found in the story of an encounter with the Pharisees. They approached Jesus and said:

> "Tell us then, what is your opinion? Is it right to pay taxes to Caesar or not?" But Jesus, knowing their evil intent, said, "You hypocrites, why are you trying to trap me? Show me the coin used for paying the tax." They brought him a denarius, and he asked them, "Whose portrait is this? And whose inscription?" "Caesar's," they replied. Then he said to them, "Give to Caesar what is Caesar's, and to God what is God's." (Matthew 22:17–21)

By arguing to give to Caesar what is Caesar's and to God what is God's, Jesus is saying that while Christians must be "in the world" and hence (for example) pay taxes and have jobs in finance, God must have a final say in how we do our daily living. If we are merely "of the world" and give to the world what the world wants (for example, in our daily work), we are leaving out of our lives the recognition that God is creator and in ultimate control of all things. Jesus implies that it is not appropriate to divide the "secular" world (such as work in banking and finance), where we do what we want, from the "religious" part. Rather, we must follow God's standards in our work and not compromise with the world, for example, by being dishonest, greedy, or self-centered in what we do.

There is a further relevant aspect of Jesus' response here, since he also highlights that Caesar's head is on the coin—an image that we know was accompanied by wording claiming Caesar to be "son of a god." Accordingly Jesus is implying that worship of money via our employment is worship of a false god—a coin bearing the image of Caesar. We are actually made in God's image, as Genesis 1:27 states:

> So God created man in his own image, in the image of God he created him; male and female he created them.

19. Indeed, Calvin maintained a ban on lending at interest to the poor; on lending that would limit our ability to give charitably; on lending that we would be unwilling to accept ourselves; on lending that does not enable the borrower to make a profit; and finally, he excludes professional lending on the ground that "whoever makes a profession of putting money out at usury, is a robber" (Graafland [2009], 4).

We owe him our very lives—and should worship him alone.

Consistent with this, Jesus was opposed to the intrusion of the commercial and financial world into the sacred realm of worship of God and relationship with him. This was illustrated in the incident of Jesus driving out the money changers from the temple:

> Jesus entered the temple area and drove out all who were buying and selling there. He overturned the tables of the money changers and the benches of those selling doves. "It is written," he said to them, "'My house will be called a house of prayer,' but you are making it a 'den of robbers.'" (Matthew 21:12–13)

Jesus, however, seems to accept as a given practice the trade of finance in the injunction in the Parable of the Talents where placing money with the bankers appears to be approved:

> You should have put my money on deposit with the bankers, so that when I returned I would have received it back with interest. (Matthew 25:27)

Though the parable may, at a deeper level, be seen as an analogy to investing in the kingdom of God.

Other aspects of Jesus' teaching can be seen as more critical of behavior typical of the financial sector. It can be argued that one aspect of Jesus' teaching is a long-term view of life, for example, the kingdom of God coming to fruition gradually like a plant growing:

> What shall we say the kingdom of God is like, or what parable shall we use to describe it? It is like a mustard seed, which is the smallest seed you plant in the ground. Yet when planted, it grows and becomes the largest of all garden plants, with such big branches that the birds of the air can perch in its shade. (Mark 4:30–32)

This stands in contrast to the practices of bankers when they focus on short-term gain to the detriment of their firms' viability. Then there is the idea of the servant that Jesus adopted as his paradigm as in Matthew 20:

> The Son of Man did not come to be served, but to serve, and to give his life as a ransom for many. (Matthew 20:28)

This model, echoed by Paul in Philippians 2, transposes into the principle that bankers should put their customers' interests first. This was clearly not the case for sellers of "toxic debt" who misled the buyers about the quality of the underlying assets.

Like the prophets, Jesus was interested in motivations, and thus encouraged honesty and plain speaking in business dealings. This is illustrated in his command:

> Simply let your "Yes" be "Yes," and your "No," "No"; anything beyond this comes from the evil one. (Matthew 5:37)

That honesty was blatantly absent for providers of "sub-prime mortgages," who misled both the borrowers[20] and those to whom the loans were sold.[21] Paul warns that:

> People who want to get rich fall into temptation and a trap. (1 Timothy 6:9)

Many bankers did exactly this when they proceeded to cut corners in the areas of prudence, diligence, and risk assessment.

On the other hand, Jesus appears to commend advance risk assessment in the case of the building of the tower and the preparation for war. For example:

> Suppose one of you wants to build a tower. Will he not first sit down and estimate the cost to see if he has enough money to complete it? For if he lays the foundation and is not able to finish it, everyone who sees it will ridicule him, saying, "This fellow began to build and was not able to finish." (Luke 14:28–30)

Though, again, the parable also represents an analogy for the kingdom of God. His followers need to be ready to pay the price in terms of suffering for following him, as he concludes in Luke 14:33, again a form of advance planning:

> In the same way, any of you who does not give up everything he has cannot be my disciple.

One aspect of the Parable of the Talents of Matthew 25:14–30, suggested by Hoare,[22] is that Jesus commends risk taking (using the

20. For example, by emphasizing the "teaser" rates (i.e., low rates of interest at the start of the loan), which gave a false impression of the long run cost of the debt.

21. By giving the false impression that due diligence had been carried out in assessing the borrowers' ability to pay when this was often not the case.

22. Hoare (2006).

talent to make more money), while the risk-averse individual (who hid his talent in the ground) is condemned. But the risk taking that is commended is ultimately for salvation, and not for financial gain. And the point should not be exaggerated; the wider setting of the parable is not so much to do with risky actions per se as obedience and faith in the context of a relationship with a master. Jesus is using contemporary illustrations to stress the critical importance of repentance and acceptance of himself as Lord of the coming kingdom.

Some of Jesus' parables contain principles that may be directly relevant to bankers' behavior, such as the parable of the shrewd manager, which we consider sufficiently important to quote here in full:

Jesus told his disciples: "There was a rich man whose manager was accused of wasting his possessions. So he called him in and asked him, 'What is this I hear about you? Give an account of your management, because you cannot be manager any longer.' The manager said to himself, 'What shall I do now? My master is taking away my job. I'm not strong enough to dig, and I'm ashamed to beg—I know what I'll do so that, when I lose my job here, people will welcome me into their houses.'

So he called in each one of his master's debtors. He asked the first, 'How much do you owe my master?' 'Eight hundred gallons of olive oil,' he replied. The manager told him, 'Take your bill, sit down quickly, and make it four hundred.' Then he asked the second, 'And how much do you owe?' 'A thousand bushels of wheat,' he replied. He told him, 'Take your bill and make it eight hundred.'

The master commended the dishonest manager because he had acted shrewdly. For the people of this world are more shrewd in dealing with their own kind than are the people of the light. I tell you, use worldly wealth to gain friends for yourselves, so that when it is gone, you will be welcomed into eternal dwellings. Whoever can be trusted with very little can also be trusted with much, and whoever is dishonest with very little will also be dishonest with much. So if you have not been trustworthy in handling worldly wealth, who will trust you with true riches? And if you have not been trustworthy with someone else's property, who will give you property of your own?

No servant can serve two masters. Either he will hate the one and love the other, or he will be devoted to the one and despise the other. You cannot serve both God and Money." (Luke 16:1–13)

Jesus commends the manager for being alert and generous (albeit with another's money) in his own long-term interests, but highlights that his problem was that he was not trustworthy. Note in this context that being trustworthy goes beyond obeying rules. It implies being honest and prudent, to be relied upon to make an appropriate judgment in the interests of the principal or client in varying situations. Similarly in today's world, trust is essential for financial markets. In fact, the root of the word "credit," namely "credere," means trust.

In Jesus' parable, the manager wasn't trustworthy beforehand, for he'd been wasting the rich man's assets, with reckless irresponsibility. This parallels the actions of some in the financial sector up to 2007. And he wasn't trustworthy in the story of the parable itself, as he gave away the master's assets. That's why Jesus calls him dishonest even as the rich man commends him for his worldly wisdom. And this is clearly relevant to banking ethics in terms of the principal-agent problem of economics as identified in section 3.1 above. Jesus appears to be saying that our trustworthiness is dependent on love and loyalty, and where they are directed. Our treasure will be where our heart is. The manager was loyal only to himself—he showed no loyalty to the rich man and so their relationship was ruptured. In the latter part of the parable, Jesus is saying—don't be dishonest like him! We can only be loyal to one master. But the manager's behavior seems very close to the economic theory model, where love and loyalty simply have no role to play. The consequences may be predictable!

Scripture calls mankind to be trustworthy to God, and we become trustworthy by being honest with money. God judges us on small things and they can have a huge effect on our destiny:

> Whoever can be trusted with very little can also be trusted with much, and whoever is dishonest with very little will also be dishonest with much. So if you have not been trustworthy in handling worldly wealth, who will trust you with true riches? (Luke 16:10–11)

One mistake that even Christians in banking can make is to compartmentalize lives, to be honest on Sunday but less trustworthy on Monday, thereby perhaps gaining a good reputation at work as a wheeler-dealer. Honesty and integrity before God can be challenged in a commercial environment, even for Christians, who can end up thinking God can't see us at all times and who get caught up in the prevailing culture because "everyone is doing it." Like the agents selling sub-prime loans to poor people in the US, knowing in their hearts they couldn't repay. They were well rewarded at the time, but their behavior was not morally acceptable.

This introduces a key verse:

> No servant can serve two masters. Either he will hate the one and love the other, or he will be devoted to the one and despise the other. You cannot serve both God and Money. (Luke 16:13)

Or in other words, you cannot serve God if your attitude to money is to see it as a goal in life, an end in itself, ultimately an idol that is worshipped, as we noted above in respect of the image of Caesar on Roman coinage.

A similar issue arose for the rich young man who had kept the law but was obsessed with his wealth:

> As Jesus started on his way, a man ran up to him and fell on his knees before him. "Good teacher," he asked, "what must I do to inherit eternal life?" "Why do you call me good?" Jesus answered. "No one is good—except God alone. You know the commandments: 'Do not murder, do not commit adultery, do not steal, do not give false testimony, do not defraud, honor your father and mother.'" "Teacher," he declared, "all these I have kept since I was a boy." Jesus looked at him and loved him. "One thing you lack," he said. "Go, sell everything you have and give to the poor, and you will have treasure in heaven. Then come, follow me." At this the man's face fell. He went away sad, because he had great wealth. Jesus looked around and said to his disciples, "How hard it is for the rich to enter the kingdom of God!" (Mark 10:17–23)

Wealth entices us into pride, selfishness, greed, and all the human motivations that mainstream economics sadly finds both accurate and predictive. God has no part in these attitudes. With the misuse of money we become only friends with ourselves, slaves trapped in spiritual poverty towards God and others, alone like King Midas amid his gold. If we trust in the "god of money" we will spend our lives in greed or fear, which are the classic motivators of investors generally. And this was what we saw in the crisis—greed of bankers and borrowers led to excessive borrowing and vulnerability, then, when there was a "shock," fear took over so lending collapsed and many banks and individuals became insolvent. Scripture is challenging all of us to observe this cycle of greed and fear in ourselves. The problem is that it is hard to see our own greed. A crisis is, in this sense, a good thing, as fear is harder to hide from. Jesus can use the crisis to show us that we are trusting in the wrong god—the god of money.

Jesus knew that one could never have a satisfactory life being in love with money.[23] And it is clear that many bankers are dissatisfied, despite their vast bonuses, with their extremely stressful lives, long hours, and resultant risk of relationship breakdown. From a biblical point of view it is unsurprising that even for people who are very highly paid, happiness and satisfaction are often absent:

> Whoever loves money never has money enough; whoever loves wealth is never satisfied with his income. This too is meaningless. (Ecclesiastes 5:11)

Instead, Jesus' call is as follows:

> "Love the Lord your God with all your heart and with all your soul and with all your mind" [Deuteronomy 6:5]. This is the first and greatest commandment. And the second is like it: "Love your neighbor as yourself" [Leviticus 19:18]. All the Law and the Prophets hang on these two commandments. (Matthew 22:37–40)

To love God and neighbor, live in community, and seek his kingdom—ironically, all are objectives contrary to the basic principles of economics that self-interest is all that counts.

In the context of the bonus culture and high remuneration of bankers, Jesus' warnings of the dangers of greed are appropriate,[24] such as in the parable of Lazarus and the rich man (Luke 16:19–31, cited on page 32). The rich man was completely oblivious to the beggar Lazarus outside his gates, in the same way that individuals who operate in impersonal markets can be blind to the individual, community, and indeed global consequences of their actions (bankruptcy, repossession,

---

23. On the breadth of Jesus' teaching on money, see Goodchild (2007), 2–6.

24. "The seven deadly sins of banking include greedy loan growth, gluttony of real estate, lust for high yields, sloth-like risk management, pride of low capital, envy of exotic fees, and anger of regulators," Mike Mayo—CLSA, April 6th 2009 (thanks to Paul Mills for sending this quote).

lost savings and pensions). And his destiny was perdition. Greed and its dangers are also highlighted in the parable of the rich fool:

> And he told them this parable: "The ground of a certain rich man produced a good crop. He thought to himself, 'What shall I do? I have no place to store my crops.' Then he said, 'This is what I'll do. I will tear down my barns and build bigger ones, and there I will store all my grain and my goods. And I'll say to myself, "You have plenty of good things laid up for many years. Take life easy; eat, drink and be merry."' But God said to him, 'You fool! This very night your life will be demanded from you. Then who will get what you have prepared for yourself?' This is how it will be with anyone who stores up things for himself but is not rich toward God." (Luke 12:16–21)

The rich fool, as in the classic economic paradigm, had only his self-interest in mind; in his greed he was focusing solely on this life and not the life to come.

A final illustration of the hubris of bankers can be seen in Revelation 18, especially the following passages that speak of the fall of Babylon, the worldly city:

> For all the nations have drunk the maddening wine of her adulteries. The kings of the earth committed adultery with her, and the merchants of the earth grew rich from her excessive luxuries . . . Give her as much torture and grief as the glory and luxury she gave herself. In her heart she boasts, "I sit as queen; I am not a widow, and I will never mourn." Therefore in one day her plagues will overtake her: death, mourning, and famine . . . The merchants of the earth will weep and mourn over her because no one buys their cargoes any more—cargoes of gold, silver, precious stones and pearls; fine linen, purple, silk and scarlet cloth; every sort of citron wood, and articles of every kind made of ivory, costly wood, bronze, iron and marble; cargoes of cinnamon and spice, of incense, myrrh and frankincense, of wine and olive oil, of fine flour and wheat; cattle and sheep; horses and carriages; and bodies and souls of men . . . The merchants who sold these things and gained their wealth from her will stand far off, terrified at her torment. They will weep and mourn and cry out: "Woe! Woe, O great city, dressed in fine linen, purple and scarlet, and glittering with gold, precious stones and pearls! In one hour such great wealth has been brought to ruin!" . . . The music of harpists and musicians, flute players and trumpeters, will never be heard in you again. No workman of any trade

will ever be found in you again. The sound of a millstone will never be heard in you again. The light of a lamp will never shine in you again. The voice of bridegroom and bride will never be heard in you again. Your merchants were the world's great men. By your magic spell all the nations were led astray. (Revelation 18:3, 7, 11–13, 15–17, 22–23)

This can be seen as depicting a financial crisis as well as a political one, with the bankers taking the place of the merchants and Babylon being the global financial sector in which all sought to work and that seemed more powerful and influential than governments. The fall of Babylon affects not only the kings of the world but also the merchants of the earth "grown rich from her excessive luxuries" (18:3), implying opulent consumerism, as in the recent boom. The merchants "will weep and mourn over her because no one buys their cargoes any more" (18:11) as did those dismissed from failing firms such as Lehman brothers. The idea that "in one hour such great wealth has been brought to ruin!" (18:17) is again reminiscent of the abrupt aggravation of the crisis at the failure of Lehmans. The succeeding recession is captured in Revelation 18:22: "No workman of any trade will ever be found in you again," while the "master of the universe" pride of the top bankers is shown in 18:23: "Your merchants were the world's great men. By your magic spell all the nations were led astray."

Higginson notes three reasons why Babylon (Revelation's code name for Rome) had to fall.[25] First, it was exploiting people (with a reference to slaves as one of the "luxury cargoes"). Second was ostentation, with all the goods being luxury ones rather than being of help to the poor. Third was pride, in parallel to the Old Testament texts proclaiming judgment on Tyre and Babylon—"In her heart she boasts, 'I sit as queen; I am not a widow, and I will never mourn'" (18:7). In a similar manner the financial sector as a whole is vulnerable to the charge of exploiting individuals' lack of information and understanding about risks. This interpretation of Revelation 18 also raises the ongoing issue of the debts of certain developing countries, incurred by dictators and of no benefit to the people, which can be seen as a form of exploitation of poor countries and peoples.

25. Higginson (1993), 198–203.

Furthermore, the ostentation of many bankers in their lifestyles and pride in their wealth and power—being seen as "masters of the universe" until 2007—have also been noteworthy and again are reminiscent of Revelation 18.

In passages such as this, biblical faith gives a warning and a challenge to the values of the world that (at least until 2007) seemed to value financial sector employment above other forms of work. Integrity is what the Bible calls for above all, as stated in Proverbs:

> The man of integrity walks securely, but he who takes crooked
> paths will be found out. (Proverbs 10:9)

This, besides being a general call to integrity in banking, can refer to the way financial crises tend to expose fraud and sharp practices that are missed in the boom but, as for Stanford and Madoff, were exposed by the downturn.

3.3 WAYS FORWARD

It is important at the outset to stress that we consider banks and modern financial markets to be essential to the modern economy. The issue, rather than their abolition, is whether they can be made to work better and whether their excesses can somehow be curbed. We contend that the crisis, following the analysis above, resulted from individual and structural causes, and both need to be addressed.

The response to the banking difficulties has been a call for the tightening of regulation, which should reduce the incentives of bankers and their shareholders to take excessive risks. This—together with the threat of takeover for banks that underperform and the threat of dismissal for individuals—is the means by which neoclassical economics envisages the way to prevent a recurrence of the current financial crisis. Regulation is typically seen in terms of capital adequacy, an appropriate remuneration system, liquidity, and internal procedures of banks. For example, the "Basel III" banking regulation envisages inter alia much higher levels of bank equity capital and liquidity in future,[26] as discussed further in Appendix 2.

---

26. Basel Committee (2011).

A first point is that while these elements are essential, forms of regulation may be too technical. They should arguably be complemented by regulation encouraging more basic "values" as benchmarks for behavior to be measured against. For example, efforts to avoid regulation by financial innovation, so-called regulatory arbitrage, could be reduced by a form of regulation forbidding actions against their spirit and not merely their letter. Featherby suggests a series of very appropriate "values" that have been neglected in finance in recent years, and which are in line with the kingdom values outlined in section 3.2 above, such as service before self, honesty and not conformity, competition and not aggression, and reward aligned with risk.[27]

Theology, with its realistic view of fallen human behavior, nevertheless raises the issue of whether even this is sufficient. Regulation (and firm culture) promoting "values" may end up with pious lists to write on the wall and ignore or seek to circumvent. In our view, a crucial complement is "virtues," which Nichols defines as "personal capacity for action, the fruit of a series of good actions, a power of progress and perfection."[28] Examples of kingdom virtues are honesty, prudence, courage, justice, trustworthiness, and diligence—the internal conviction of what is right behavior and determination to follow it through. Gregg suggests that the most important of these is prudence, "the perfected ability of individuals possessing right freedom and free will to make morally correct practical decisions," [29] for example, using experience, data, and judgment in the granting of credit.[30] And we highlighted in section 3.2 above that this is precisely the behavior that Scripture requires.

Hence, the question arises how and whether bankers can be motivated to follow prudence, integrity, and business ethics.[31] How can we instill kingdom virtues? How can banking structures be developed to encourage good people to do the good they want to do? One aspect

27. Featherby (2009), 17–19.

28. Nichols (2008).

29. Gregg (2010), 48.

30. Gregg (2010) goes on to see the parts of prudence as "understanding of first principles (e.g., 'don't steal'), open-mindedness, humility, caution, the willingness to research alternative possibilities, foresight, shrewdness, and the capacity to form an accurate sense of the reality of situations."

31. See Green (1988), 120–35.

is that firms could be encouraged to reward such virtues financially wherever they are found. The church can point out that moral behavior is a sine qua non for the modern economy to function, with all the benefits it provides. Christians in finance can act as examples, especially if they are leaders. For virtue depends on character and character is learned by example rather than precept.

For example, the global bank HSBC was led during the crisis by Stephen Green, who is a Christian and indeed an ordained Anglican minister. That bank emerged relatively unscathed, which we contend was not a coincidence since his approach clearly was a more prudent one than that of his contemporaries. It is clear that Christians such as Green are not called to leave the financial sector but must become "salt and light" by the virtues they display, in the place where God has called them to his service, "working for the Lord and not for men." The force of example and careful lifestyle evangelism can pay dividends for the firm as well as leading individuals to salvation.

But perhaps fundamental to reestablishment of ethical behavior may be the resolution of the question of who is the ultimate master: you, the employer, or God? Perhaps only when God is in charge of their lives will bankers see the incongruity of taxpayer support for their institutions and recurrence of large bonuses. Then they will see the injustice of it, given taxpayers are on average far poorer than the average banker.

We accept that virtues cannot be relied on alone—some people will always lack virtue and need regulations and values to be measured against. Values are enforceable while virtues are not—so they are needed as a backup. But we contend that a financial system that neither promotes nor rewards such virtue has the seeds of its own destruction.

From a secular viewpoint, another way to limit losses via "disaster myopia" is to retain older bankers with corporate memory and experience of past crises—otherwise the same mistakes tend to be made again. This has not tended to happen in practice, as older bankers are often made redundant, leaving in charge younger individuals with no memory of crisis. The Bible could be quoted in favor of this in terms of the good advice Rehoboam son of Solomon received from his elderly advisors (1 Kings 12), to reconcile himself with his restless subjects by easing their burden of tax and forced labor.

> Then King Rehoboam consulted the elders who had served his father Solomon during his lifetime. "How would you advise me to answer these people?" he asked. They replied, "If today you will be a servant to these people and serve them and give them a favorable answer, they will always be your servants." But Rehoboam rejected the advice the elders gave him and consulted the young men who had grown up with him and were serving him. He asked them, "What is your advice? How should we answer these people who say to me, 'Lighten the yoke your father put on us'?" The young men who had grown up with him replied, "Tell these people who have said to you, 'Your father put a heavy yoke on us, but make our yoke lighter'—tell them, 'My little finger is thicker than my father's waist. My father laid on you a heavy yoke; I will make it even heavier. My father scourged you with whips; I will scourge you with scorpions.'"
> (1 Kings 12:6–11)

In fact he took his young friends' bad advice, to "act tough," and prompted the breakup of the kingdom.

A further policy to pursue is to reduce moral hazard from the "safety net" that generates incentives to act imprudently, as discussed in chapter 5, section 3.

It is clear that something has gone badly wrong for banks to in effect create the deepest recession since the 1930s. This raises the question whether banks, which were devised for the good of the community, have become self-seeking and destructive. A biblical analysis could support an enforced decline in the importance and influence of the financial sector.

For example, in the words of Archbishop of Canterbury, Rowan Williams, it is easy to personify the market and capital "as if they were individuals, with purposes and strategies, making choices, deliberating reasonably about how to achieve aims. We lose sight of the fact that they are things that we make. They are sets of practices, habits, agreements which have arisen through a mixture of choice and chance." And so "we expect an abstraction called 'the market' to produce the common good or to regulate its potential excesses by a sort of natural innate prudence, like a physical organism or ecosystem. We appeal to 'business' to acquire public responsibility and moral vision."[32] Indeed, this is what the Bible calls idolatry, attributing agency to something

32. Williams (2008).

we have made ourselves—and hence there is a need for discernment to avoid the risk of structural evil that such abstraction can lead us to. It can lead to foolish and destructive errors about the self-stabilizing nature of the economy or financial system, for example.[33] Such idolatry is also a way for individuals to seek to avoid responsibility by blaming the system or the institution when there were alternative choices that such individuals could have made.

Besides our attitude to it, the size of the financial sector could also be questioned. We have noted that Calvin suggested that banking transactions between equal parties were unexceptionable, under Jesus' law of love. In general we can agree with Calvin that much lending is beneficial to society. In our view, if all transactions were equity-based as opposed to many being debt-based then there would be a collapse in economic activity (although Mills makes a strong argument for a switch to equity-based finance[34]).

Regardless of the view taken on this point, there could remain questions on the value added by banking and finance (is it all beneficial or partly "parasitic" on the real economy?). For example, there could be questions about the value of the myriad of derivative transactions, some of which may be for hedging but many of which are purely speculative, such as credit default swaps on structured products. It is intriguing that the head of the UK regulatory authority, the Financial Services Authority (FSA),[35] Lord Turner, has raised the issue of a transactions tax on financial trading that would reduce the scope of such speculation and would likely reduce the overall size of the financial sector. Others have argued to break up the monopoly power of large banks, which also threatens financial stability. This, it can be argued, is in line with the implication of Revelation 18, that the "Babylon" of

33. Such beliefs, common among economists, are in fact contrary to the teachings of the greatest economists of the past, such as Keynes (1936), 159, who said, "Speculation may do no harm as bubbles on a steady stream of enterprise. The position is serious when enterprise becomes a bubble on the whirlpool of speculation. When the economic development of a country is a by-product of the activities of a casino (i.e., the financial markets) the job is likely to be ill done."

34. Mills (2011).

35. The FSA has since been split up and its prudential supervisory responsibility now lies with the Bank of England.

the financial sector had become too powerful and influential for the economies it should serve.

Some legislation has been passed that moves in this direction. In the US, the Dodd-Frank Act imposed a prohibition on most proprietary trading by US banks and their affiliates, subject to limited exceptions, and restricts covered institutions from owning, sponsoring, or investing in hedge funds or private equity funds.[36] The UK government has announced that there will be ring-fencing of retail banking operations from investment banking in conglomerates. This is intended to ensure that if UK banks get into difficulty with their investment banking operations, the bank for ordinary consumers will be protected and the investment banking arm can be allowed to fail. The UK government has, however, stopped short of breaking up the banks, as was suggested at an earlier stage.

Calvin might well agree with such policies, quite apart from condemning as contrary to the "law of love" the more predatory lending to sub-prime borrowers (many of whom have lost their houses due to repossession), as well as doorstep selling of high-interest products by financial salespersons in poor communities. Indeed, the impersonality of the market, especially when structured products break the lender/borrower link, suggests a need to make finance once again more a question of personal relationships—in line with Scripture, where, as emphasized in section 2.2, the doctrine of the Trinity teaches that God is relational, so human beings, made in his image, are inevitably relational also. Moral hazard is reduced in close relationships, as in the household of biblical times where people could monitor one another closely, and also in "microlending" in developing countries, where there is peer monitoring of use of the loan by groups of local people (who get a loan in rotation) and lending to women, who are usually more responsible than men.[37] In this context, after the crisis of

36. Among other key provisions, the Act has introduced a new regulatory regime for the over-the-counter derivatives market. In order to increase transparency, liquidity, and efficiency, these markets will be subject to clearing and exchange trading, as well as a number of other requirements. Similarly, under the Act, issuers or originators of asset-backed securities will be required to retain at least 5 percent of the credit risk associated with the assets that they sell into a securitization. Meanwhile, in order to reduce conflicts of interest and promote transparency, credit rating agencies will also be given new corporate governance guidelines.

37. The Grameen Bank in Bangladesh is a key example. See Bornstein (2005).

the early 1990s, a common belief in Sweden is that banks went astray when "they stopped lending only to those they could see from the church tower."

The downside of lending to relatively few customers, with whom one has close relationships (possibly in a small geographic area), is lack of diversification in a bank's portfolio of loans. However, greater stability and lower default rates may more than offset this.

To ensure a "level playing field" between bankers and their customers there is also a need for enhancing the understanding of financial products by individuals. This may require regulation of complexity, i.e., not permitting products to be marketed that are judged too complex for retail consumers to understand. It also requires training of all individuals in finance, which could be undertaken by churches as discussed in chapter 4, section 3 below.

Chapter 4

The Household Sector— Private Debt

4.1 FROM AN ECONOMICS PERSPECTIVE

Although we highlight in chapter 1 and Appendix 1 that there are common features linking this crisis to those of the past, the importance of household sector debt has been an outstanding feature, which was less marked in historic crises.[1] Nonfinancial companies, other than in commercial property, have generally been more circumspect in borrowing in recent years than in past credit booms. This point, and the social issues raised by household debt, make it essential to assess this topic in detail.

It is self-evident that although bankers bear some of the responsibility for the crisis, the household sector was not obliged to take on massive debt burdens. In other words, they—we—were complicit in the process of overlending, indeed celebrating the house price and consumer boom. Hence, we now go on to analyze the financial behavior of households in countries such as the US and UK.

In both the US and the UK debt burdens are very high, although they have fallen since 2008 due to debt repayment and default. In March 2011, the average American household carried $7,394 in credit

1. Davis (1995), chs. 6 and 8, provides accounts of historic crises.

card debt, although among households with credit cards the figure was much higher at $14,743.[2] Total debt including mortgages was $43,874 per person and $117,951 per household in 2010.[3] One third of EU consumer debt is in the UK. In April 2011, every UK household bore on average £8,121 in consumer debt (£15,618 for those having any unsecured debt) and £55,815 including mortgage debt,[4] far above the EU average in each case. The debt-household income ratio in both the US and UK stood well over 100 percent. There seems to be a difference in behavior more widely between "Anglo Saxon" countries such as the US, UK, Ireland, and Australia, and the continent of Europe and East Asia. Households in the former are much more willing to incur debt—and the banks much more willing to lend to them.

As noted in chapter 2, from an economic viewpoint, individuals are universally assumed to wish to maximize their own lifetime consumption, and minimize work as opposed to leisure. Over a lifetime, there are periods when income is low (when studying, early in career and in retirement) and others when income is high (in middle age). Although lifetime consumption maximization does not require it, rational individuals are also assumed by economists to seek to minimize volatility in consumption (e.g., collapse of consumption in old age, low consumption in young adulthood). Stability of consumption improves utility overall if, as is commonly assumed, there is diminishing marginal utility of consumption (an extra unit of consumption when it is already high is worth less to an individual than an extra unit at low levels of consumption). Then, the so-called life cycle paradigm most commonly adopted by economists states that, the consumer does (and should) rationally carry out "intertemporal optimization" or "smoothing" to boost consumption when it is low.

Given a normal income profile (i.e., with income rising over time and heavy expenditure on household formation in young adulthood), such smoothing is likely to mean heavy borrowing early in the life cycle and corresponding repayments later. Borrowing may be implicitly

2. Source: http://www.creditcards.com/credit-card-news/credit-card-industry-facts-personal-debt-statistics-1276.php

3. Source: http://www.visualeconomics.com/the-american-familys-financial-turmoil_2010-04-29/

4. Source: Moneybasics: http://www.moneybasics.co.uk/en/resources/money_information.html

against the security of human wealth (consumer credit against future wage income) or explicitly against nonhuman wealth (such as mortgages on property). Correspondingly, as regards purpose, the borrowing may be directly for consumption or indirectly for the purchase of investment goods or durables (house, car, domestic appliances) that provide a stream of consumption services. As income rises, borrowing is repaid and people save in middle age for retirement. This saving is then decumulated as a pension when the person is in retirement and other income is low.

Growth in income and asset prices may raise the amount of borrowing in an optimal life cycle pattern of income, consumption, and saving. A growing real income increases the residual part of income over and above necessities that can be devoted to interest payments, while growing wealth increases collateral for debt. Note that there is no reference in economic analysis of the "life cycle" to the wider implications of accumulating wealth, which are linked to independence, security, status, and power. Nor does it refer to the risk of debt.

If there are constraints on borrowing due, for example, to restrictive regulation of bank lending, this may, of course, affect the amount of borrowing relative to an optimal life cycle pattern. In this case, consumers are said to be "liquidity constrained" and their consumption will be closely tied to receipts of income, though assets will also be available to decumulate for consumption. Such liquidity constraints typically imply that households cannot consume at the level defined by their lifetime consumption plan at the points where heavy borrowing would be required early in the life span. This is seen as undesirable by economists, as such liquidity constraints imply that constrained consumers incur welfare losses owing to low consumption in early adulthood, even though consumption can be made up later in the life cycle. In other words, limits on lending mean consumption is more volatile over the life cycle than if borrowing were freely permitted. This argument was part of the background for the widespread policy advice to deregulate credit markets and remove any controls on bank lending, which was implemented in the Reagan/Thatcher years of the 1980s.

Any such loosening of lending constraints will tend to be marked by a sharply rising household debt/income and (to a lesser degree) debt/wealth ratio, as well as a reduction in the proportion of income that is saved, as observed in the US and UK since the 1980s, as households adjust towards their optimal level of consumption. In those countries, financial liberalization in the 1980s was the key step in easing of liquidity constraints, notably by increasing competition in the mortgage market. But a further step more recently was securitization and development of global wholesale financial markets, which enabled banks to raise far larger volumes of funds for mortgage lending than hitherto, with fewer restrictions. (For example, in the UK, Northern Rock offered loans of 125 percent of property values.) Note again that such a release of constraints was generally seen as a positive development by economists, since it enables consumers better to smooth their consumption.

An important aspect overlaying the life cycle in the US and UK is the behavior of the residential property market. It may itself impose dynamics on the pattern of demand for borrowing. In particular, researchers such as Hendry[5] and Muellbauer and Murphy[6] have found evidence of "frenzies" where rising real estate prices enter a spiral with demand for mortgages, partly driven by fear of being left behind, on the part of first-time buyers. This implies that at times rising prices may induce purchases purely intended for profit by resale. There was clearly an element of speculation in some house purchases in the recent boom, notably in the US from "flipping" of apartments[7] and in the UK from buy-to-let, further boosting indebtedness. The counterpart may be sharp reductions in real estate prices following such frenzies, as seen in the current crisis.

Going beyond this, it is acknowledged by economists that individuals have some tendency to prefer consumption today to that in the future (this is called "pure time preference"). This propensity may be due to myopia, with people being unable to envisage the future; finite human lives; risks to any form of saving from, for instance, inflation or a stock market crash; and the expectation to benefit from the growth of the economy as a whole. The tendency to prefer consumption today may offset the seeming rationality of the life cycle, leading

5. Hendry (1984).

6. Muellbauer and Murphy (1991).

7. Flipping is a term used primarily in the United States to describe purchasing a revenue-generating asset and quickly reselling (or "flipping") it for profit. Though flipping can apply to any asset, the term is most often applied to real estate and initial public offerings.

people to go into debt beyond the level needed for constant consumption over a lifetime, so that people "enjoy today and suffer tomorrow." On the other hand, a countervailing factor should be the interest rate on deposits (or return on other assets) that encourages saving today over consumption.

The current working generation in the US and the UK appears to be unusually affected by the short-termist tendency to consume more than is consistent with lifetime optimization. Indeed, focusing on the UK, economists Barrell and Weale characterize a "profligate cohort," aged roughly 25–45 in the early 2000s, whose behavior has followed this pattern.[8] They have borrowed massively for consumption, both via consumer credit itself and by mortgage lending that is actually used for consumption (housing equity extraction loans). They do not appear to be saving sufficiently for a comfortable retirement. Similarly in the US, there has been widespread home equity extraction for consumption and this has contributed to the rise in debt. Furthermore, 40 percent of working Americans are not saving for retirement and 25 percent have no savings at all.[9] Profligate behavior in this sense is, of course, facilitated by the free access to credit in the US and UK financial system. This pattern is not observed in countries such as Germany, France, and Italy, where saving is much higher and borrowing much less—and where household borrowing is much more restricted by the banks.

The expectation of rising house prices is probably more engrained in the UK than the US, while public pensions are much less generous. Accordingly, whereas US individuals who have not saved in financial assets can look forward to relatively generous social security pensions, it may be that this generation in the UK who are not saving in pension funds, expects that rising house prices will "bail them out" by providing sufficient assets to retire on. But real estate prices may well come under further downward pressure in coming decades when the current large baby boom generation retires. And meanwhile, as discussed in chapter 5, the state of public finances leaves little room for an expanded social security pension scheme in the UK, even abstracting from the "ageing of the population." And social security pensions in the US

8. Barrell and Weale (2009), 109.

9. Source: http://www.visualeconomics.com/the-american-familys-financial
-turmoil_2010-04-29/

are under threat from the state of public finances also. If these points are correct, then low consumption in retirement will be the long-term downside of high debt for recent borrowers.

The shorter-term downside of free availability of debt is, of course, risk of having to default, entailing loss of property, income, or credit standing. Default risk is dependent not merely on debt or income but also on the other assets in the balance sheet of the borrowers and macroeconomic variables such as interest rates and the economic cycle, which are beyond the borrower's control. The question is how vulnerable individuals allow themselves to be to such shocks, and also whether people misperceive likely future income growth or their employment security. Economic analysis of default is assumed to be based on simple cost and benefit analysis by individuals; costs of default to households may include financial penalties and also restricted access to credit in the future. It is not seen as a matter of moral judgment. Meanwhile, even if consumers do not default, periods when there are negative shocks to income or interest rates[10] will lead to much lower consumption than is desired since the burden of repaying interest and principal comes to preempt a large proportion of income.

If they are rational, lenders should charge higher interest rates on loans with higher credit risk or ration credit, for example, by requiring lower loan-to-value ratios on mortgages to allow for the possibility of default. But in the recent boom, lenders to buy-to-let, sub-prime, and even conventional lenders appear to have been careless about borrower risk, focusing only on initial returns rather than long-term ability to repay. As noted above, this may link to the fact that loans were often securitized and hence the initial lender did not bear the default risk.

There are, of course, differences between consumer credit and mortgage credit in terms of risk. Collateral for house purchase is immediately available in the form of the title deeds to the property. Compared with consumer credit, the risk to the lender relates to the risk that, owing to regional or national depression, the value of the collateral will have fallen below the outstanding principal of the loan, in which case the borrower may have an incentive to default. There are obviously also transactions costs to foreclosure. Accordingly, the

10. We note that an unusual feature of the recent mortgage boom in the US was the high proportion of adjustable rate mortgages, which would be strongly affected by rises in general rates.

risk of a default leading to a loss for a lending institution is greater the greater the proportion of a household's debt that is constituted by unsecured consumer lending. But this is reflected in higher interest rates on credit card lending.

In practice, greater quantitative losses have been made on mortgage credit, perhaps because the lower default rate makes lenders complacent about absolute risks to balance sheets arising from credit risk in real estate loans. Also in much of the US, the scope for borrowers to default is much greater since mortgage loans are "nonrecourse" and the household's liability is limited to the value of the property. This is not the case in the UK or elsewhere in Europe where a mortgage default in the case of negative equity entails a lien on the borrower's income. Individuals who default on their mortgages remain liable, in other words, even if they "hand in the keys" to the lender.

To sum up, economics offers an understanding of the behavior of households in the recent crisis, but there remain puzzles from the point of view of the "rational economic humanity" paradigm. For example, why did so many households irrationally borrow in excess of their presumed lifecycle optimum, threatening loan default and repossession in the short run and a poor pension in the long run? Why was such a value placed on consumption "now" that saving was neglected? We now turn to a theological point of view to seek further insights.

4.2 FROM A THEOLOGICAL PERSPECTIVE

The starting point in assessing a biblical view of household debt is to consider its objective, namely consumption (including the consumption of housing services). And we must start by pointing out that the Bible does not deny the goodness of God's creation that is available for humankind's enjoyment and indeed consumption. Jesus, for example, enjoyed good meals, being accused of being a "glutton and a drunkard" (Matthew 11:19), producing miraculously the finest wine at the wedding at Cana, thus indeed foreshadowing the Wedding Supper that will await the righteous in the new heaven and the new earth (Revelation 19:9).

Nevertheless, as we noted in chapter 2, section 2 above, wealth and consumption in themselves should not be core to human life. The quality of relationships with others and with God should be more important. Furthermore, the Bible is replete with warnings against excess in consumption. For example, Jesus warns his followers to

> Be on your guard against all kinds of greed; a man's life does not consist in the abundance of his possessions. (Luke 12:15).

And Paul warns that

> People who want to get rich fall into temptation and a trap and into many foolish and harmful desires that plunge men into ruin and destruction. For the love of money is a root of all kinds of evil. Some people, eager for money, have wandered from the faith and pierced themselves with many griefs (1 Timothy 6:9–10).

Note that Paul is saying there is a risk of loss of faith as well as financial ruin arising from desire to be rich.

Scripture contends that there is a need to exercise moderation in consumption, being content with what you have,[11] as is shown by, for example, the book of Proverbs.

> Do not wear yourself out to get rich; have the wisdom to show restraint. (Proverbs 23:4)

> If you find honey, eat just enough—too much of it, and you will vomit. (Proverbs 25:16)

The wise person is warned in Proverbs to get income first before consuming, implying the priority of saving over borrowing, a tradition that has all but died out in the US and UK:

> Finish your outdoor work and get your fields ready; after that, build your house. (Proverbs 24:27)

Sider,[12] arguing for a simpler lifestyle, endorses John Wesley, who argued that the solution for a rich Christian is to give away all income except what is needed for "the plain necessaries of life," while nonetheless maintaining capital and accumulating it further as necessary.[13] One basis is the command in Hebrews:

> Keep your lives free from the love of money and be content with what you have, because God has said, "Never will I leave you; never will I forsake you." (Hebrews 13:5)

11. See also Beaudoin (2003).
12. Sider (1997), 189–208.
13. Wesley (1996), 1

For Sider, the barrier to such simplicity is the "unprecedented material luxuries" of Western societies that too quickly becomes necessities. This may entail what is called "spiritual poverty" based on addiction to consumption and entailing unwillingness to give any income away either to God or the poor.

Households in the US and UK evidently disregarded such advice for a simpler lifestyle, borrowing heavily to consume in excess of their income. Accordingly, biblically as well as economically, the blame for current debt problems cannot be laid solely with bankers; all of us need to apply the following saying of Jesus to our view of the bankers:

> Do not judge or you too will be judged. (Matthew 7:1)

Households freely took out large loans with a view to profiting in the short term from higher house prices, extracting equity for consumption or living in homes beyond their means. These loans have become a millstone for many, as house prices have fallen below the value of mortgages (negative equity) or income is insufficient to pay interest on the debt. Over the long term, heavy debt repayments will hinder ability to save for retirement, a prudential activity that many households appear in any case to have abandoned.

We note that excessive consumption and debt is not only of concern for the risk it gives to households' future well-being but also for its side effects on the environment and on the poor. There is also the issue whether consumption and GDP are good measures of happiness, health, and well-being.[14] We do not focus on these issues in this book.

The irrationality of recent consumer behavior is perhaps less of a surprise to theology than to economics, in the sense that a generation that disowns its creator, following on from the fall, is not likely to act in its own long-term interests either:

> The fool says in his heart, "There is no God." They are corrupt,
> and their ways are vile; there is no one who does good. (Psalm
> 53:1)

Rejection of God may itself be linked to wealth, as Solomon implies in Proverbs 30:8:

---

14. See SDC (2009).

> Keep falsehood and lies far from me; give me neither poverty
> nor riches, but give me only my daily bread. Otherwise, I may
> have too much and disown you and say, "Who is the Lord?"

The Bible is replete with warnings about debt. A key aspect is of
"binding the future," in the sense that debt limits the flexibility we
have in life, and hence the liberty God intends us to have as stewards
of creation. It can ultimately lead to a form of slavery, as was the case
for the Egyptian farmers during the famine who had to give up their
land to Pharaoh in exchange for food:

> The Egyptians, one and all, sold their fields, because the fam-
> ine was too severe for them. The land became Pharaoh's, and
> Joseph reduced the people to servitude, from one end of Egypt
> to the other. (Genesis 47:20–21)

Equally in Nehemiah 5:1–5, the Israelites were forced to go into debt,
or sell their children into slavery to obtain food from the rich or to
pay taxes to the king.

> Now the men and their wives raised a great outcry against
> their Jewish brothers. Some were saying, "We and our sons and
> daughters are numerous; in order for us to eat and stay alive,
> we must get grain." Others were saying, "We are mortgaging
> our fields, our vineyards, and our homes to get grain during the
> famine." Still others were saying, "We have had to borrow mon-
> ey to pay the king's tax on our fields and vineyards. Although
> we are of the same flesh and blood as our countrymen and
> though our sons are as good as theirs, yet we have to subject
> our sons and daughters to slavery. Some of our daughters have
> already been enslaved, but we are powerless, because our fields
> and our vineyards belong to others."

There is a biblical parallel between debt and sin, given that both
are enslaving and destructive if not covered and eliminated. This is
seen when we compare the Lord's Prayer in Luke 11:4, which states,
"forgive us our sins" with Matthew 6:12, "forgive us our debts." Peter
Selby argues that debt closes down the possibility of the future in both
Old and New Testaments, and hence the potential of the Christian
life.[15] For example, we will find it hard to accept a call from God to

15. Selby (1997), 66–69.

move into lower paid employment, such as in pastoral ministry, that furthers the kingdom. Recall that Luke 9:57–62 states:

> As they were walking along the road, a man said to him, "I will follow you wherever you go." Jesus replied, "Foxes have holes and birds of the air have nests, but the Son of Man has no place to lay his head."
>
> He said to another man, "Follow me." But the man replied, "Lord, first let me go and bury my father." Jesus said to him, "Let the dead bury their own dead, but you go and proclaim the kingdom of God."
>
> Still another said, "I will follow you, Lord; but first let me go back and say good-by to my family." Jesus replied, "No one who puts his hand to the plow and looks back is fit for service in the kingdom of God."

Rather than saying "I have to bury my father" or "I have to say good-by to my family," today's excuse for not following a call from Jesus is likely to be "I have to pay off the mortgage first." Equally, our scope for giving to the poor is limited when high debts pre-empt much of our income.

The Bible also warns about getting into debt voluntarily, pointing out that:

> the borrower is servant to the lender. (Proverbs 22:7)

This form of slavery arises from the obligation to repay the debt we have incurred; we spend much of our working time doing so, rather than being free to spend our income as we receive it. And at a deeper level, Jesus has paid for our debts to God by dying for us on the cross. God wants us to be free of all debts, except the debt of gratitude to Jesus for what he has done to us. That is why Paul writes:

> You were bought at a price, do not become slaves to men.
> (1 Corinthians 7:23)

God's generosity in freeing us from our debt to him through sin is also the core point of the king's generosity in Jesus' parable of the unmerciful servant:

> Therefore, the kingdom of heaven is like a king who wanted to settle accounts with his servants. As he began the settlement, a man who owed him ten thousand talents was brought to him.

> Since he was not able to pay, the master ordered that he and his wife and his children and all that he had be sold to repay the debt. The servant fell on his knees before him. "Be patient with me," he begged, "and I will pay back everything." The servant's master took pity on him, canceled the debt and let him go. (Matthew 18:23–27)

How then can we choose voluntarily to be indebted?

Habakkuk gives warnings about speculation and use of borrowed funds to enhance standards of living, as he states:

> Woe to him who piles up stolen goods and makes himself wealthy by extortion! How long must this go on? Will not your debtors suddenly arise? Will they not wake up and make you tremble? Then you will become their victim. (Habakkuk 2:6–7)

This might arise, for example, if the assets bought with borrowed funds fall in value, as in the case of highly leveraged housing loans. There are also widespread warnings about guaranteeing debts for others, as in Proverbs:

> Do not be a man who strikes hands in pledge or puts up security for debts; if you lack the means to pay, your very bed will be snatched from under you. (Proverbs 22:26–27)

This is not only due to the risk of financial loss, but also because the borrower is likely to be borrowing beyond his or her means if such an arrangement is needed. Furthermore, the relationship of the borrower to the cosigner is at risk in this case.[16]

There are widespread provisions for writing off debt in the Bible, although they typically assume that the borrower is poor and the loan was taken on involuntarily owing to adverse financial circumstances rather than, as in recent years, a voluntary transaction motivated by speculation or desire for a higher living standard. And it is not clear they were ever instituted in practice. The Jubilee every forty-nine years was to allow for periodic return of land to the family that originally owned it, who may have had to sell it to pay off debt (Leviticus 25:23–28, see page 30). The Sabbath year every seven years entailed release of debts except those due from foreigners, stating simply:

---

16. See also Proverbs 11:15, "He who puts up security for another will surely suffer, but whoever refuses to strike hands in pledge is safe."

> At the end of every seven years you must cancel debts.
> (Deuteronomy 15:1)

Other provisions of the Sabbath year include freedom of Hebrew slaves and land left fallow to recover from crop-bearing. In these provisions God overrides unlimited property rights for the rich with his own higher compassionate justice, since he is the "maker of all things" (Ecclesiastes 11:5).

More broadly, by such provisions, God creates a mechanism of "structural justice," giving rise to entitlements for the poor, to offset the tendency of fallen humankind to exploit others' misfortunes. As noted, Matthew's version of the Lord's prayer asks God to

> forgive us our debts, as we also have forgiven our debtors.
> (Matthew 6:12)

Paul urges the Christians in Rome to

> Let no debt remain outstanding, except the continuing debt to love one another, for he who loves his fellow man has fulfilled the law. (Romans 13:8)

Honoring one's obligations to others is discussed further below.

Selby argues that the Nunc Dimittis of Simeon in Luke 2:25–35[17] is related to releasing a slave from the past, akin to releasing a debtor, in the context of the broad theme of redemption.[18] Similarly, banks and legal debt processes may need to offer debt forgiveness to those in consumer debt beyond their ability to repay, or at least offer interest holidays or extended repayment periods for mortgage borrowers to give them more time to repay.

A wider obligation rests on Christians to care for the needy, who cannot sustain consumption due to shocks—or following their own financial errors.[19] We are commanded to give to those who have immediate acute needs from hunger and lack of clothing and shelter as do charities:

17. See especially Luke 2:28–32: "Simeon took him in his arms and praised God, saying: 'Sovereign Lord, as you have promised, you now dismiss your servant in peace. For my eyes have seen your salvation, which you have prepared in the sight of all people, a light for revelation to the Gentiles and for glory to your people Israel.'"

18. Selby (1997), 95.

19. Ibid., 69–72.

> If anyone has material possessions and sees his brother in need
> but has no pity on him, how can the love of God be in him? (1
> John 3:17)

But at other times lending is seen as an appropriate response:

> If there is a poor man among your brothers . . . freely lend him
> whatever he needs. (Deuteronomy 15:7–8)

This is because lending to those in need enables individuals to maintain self-respect, to acknowledge their responsibility to care for themselves, and to affirm desire and hope to repay. Meanwhile the lender
must act as God would, being willing to forgive debts. Jesus is quite
explicit in this regard:[20]

> And if you lend to those from whom you expect repayment,
> what credit is that to you? Even "sinners" lend to "sinners,"
> expecting to be repaid in full. But love your enemies, do good
> to them, and lend to them without expecting to get anything
> back. (Luke 6:34–35)

This point does not extend to those still able to repay their debts
but refusing to do so. For them, the Bible stresses taking responsibility for actions—there is an obligation on borrowers to repay debts incurred, if their incomes are sufficient:

> The wicked borrow and do not repay, but the righteous give
> generously. (Psalm 37:21)

The fact that the Bible accepts the use of collateral, using the term
"security" or "pledge," implies an expectation of repayment, as for example Deuteronomy states:

> Do not take a pair of millstones—not even the upper one—as
> security for a debt, because that would be taking a man's liveli-
> hood as security. (Deuteronomy 24:6)

> Stay outside and let the man to whom you are making the loan
> bring the pledge out to you. (Deuteronomy 24:11)

---

20. Calvin argues that this passage does not condemn interest altogether. Christ
did not intend to regulate lending, but rather wanted to fight the natural tendency
of human beings to be slow in helping others, because they are accustomed to look
at profitable ways of investing their money (Graafland [2009], 3).

A corollary is that bankruptcy should not be seen as an easy option, and especially not if the borrower knew from the time of borrowing that their finances were overstretched. Even if he or she is forced into involuntary bankruptcy, the Scriptures enjoin keeping one's word, for example, Jesus' teaching:

> Simply let your "Yes" be "Yes," and your "No," "No"; anything beyond this comes from the evil one. (Matthew 5:37)

So there could be an attempt to make amends for earlier losses for the lender once the borrower's financial situation improves.

These passages have a bearing on the practice of "strategic default" that is common in the US, of defaulting on mortgages simply when there is negative equity whereas there are no repayment difficulties. Such strategic default would be impossible elsewhere in the world, since outside the US there is recourse of the lender to the income of the borrower and not just the value of the collateral.[21] Whereas Deuteronomy 24:6 and 11 cited above could be seen as implying that the collateral should be sufficient to protect the lender, Psalm 37:21 and Matthew 5:37 imply it is "wicked" not to repay and thus to fail to keep one's word. Consideration of the negative impact of foreclosure on the prices of neighboring properties tends to underpin this point.[22]

Responsible behavior also includes avoiding the need for assistance if it lies within our means. For example, we have seen that a corollary of the debt binge was inadequate saving for pensions and a risk of being a burden on others via social security and poverty relief. Paul warns Christians about becoming deliberately dependent:

> For even when we were with you, we gave you this rule: "If a man will not work, he shall not eat." We hear that some among you are idle. They are not busy; they are busybodies. Such people we command and urge in the Lord Jesus Christ to settle down and earn the bread they eat. (2 Thessalonians 3:10–12)

21. Harris (2010), 13.

22. According to FDIC (2011), 2, and based on research dating from 2005, (1) homes in foreclosure that become vacant provide sites for crime or other neighborhood problems. One foreclosure can impose up to $34,000 in direct costs on local government agencies, including inspections, court actions, police, and fire department efforts, potential demolition, unpaid water and sewage, and trash removal. (2) One foreclosure can result in as much as an additional $220,000 in reduced property value and home equity for nearby homes.

On this basis, the "profligate cohort" seemingly relying on house prices, social security, and the generosity of their own offspring to bail them out is acting irresponsibly. James 4:13–17,[23] besides illustrating the arrogance of bankers, is relevant to the "presumption on the future" that not saving sufficiently entails.

The command to write off debts after seven years in Deuteronomy 15:1 is also a limit on the duration of debts, assuming the lender wanted to retrieve his assets. The lender was to know that if he loaned money that could not reasonably be repaid within the seven years, this would be written off. Accordingly, the lender would be incentivized to care for the long-term best interests of the borrower, where the latter is assumed to be in a position of relative weakness. While we do not advocate a seven-year biblical limit, there are important general lessons. Not lending too much and being willing to extend terms in case of difficulty are among the responses that lenders should adopt in this context.

We note that with free availability of credit, houses may be priced out of the reach of those on low income, i.e., there are external effects as well as direct effects of individual debt. This can be related to the prophetic concern about land holdings and poverty in the Old Testament, where individuals become destitute after losing their land. It could be personal, as in the case of seizure of land from the poor and stealing land by moving boundary markers:

> They covet fields and seize them, and houses, and take them. They defraud a man of his home, a fellowman of his inheritance. (Micah 2:2)

> Do not move an ancient boundary stone or encroach on the fields of the fatherless. (Proverbs 23:10)

But it could also be "structural" as in the case of legalized oppression of the poor, a corrupt legal system, and unjust decrees favoring the rich, leading in turn to concentration of land holdings:

> Woe to those who make unjust laws, to those who issue oppressive decrees, to deprive the poor of their rights and withhold justice from the oppressed of my people, making widows their prey and robbing the fatherless. (Isaiah 10:1–2)

23. Quoted on p. 40.

> Woe to you who add house to house and join field to field till no
> space is left and you live alone in the land. (Isaiah 5:8)

It is clear that, notably in the UK, there is an upcoming generation who have lost out massively from the housing bubble simply because they now cannot afford houses and are having to rent or stay
with parents (as well as being burdened with much more student debt
than their forebears). All of this is redolent of injustice. Even with the
falls in UK house prices to date, real estate remains very expensive relative to average income, although in the US houses are more afford-
able. The older generation and the banks bear some responsibility for
this, although some parents of sufficient means are taking responsibility by helping their offspring to get on the housing ladder. A further
fall in UK house prices would help resolve the situation, naturally at a
cost to current indebted homeowners.

On the positive side of debt is the underlying biblical value of
having property/housing, as in the peaceful and prosperous future en-
visaged by Micah:

> Every man will sit under his own vine and under his own fig
> tree, and no one will make them afraid, for the Lord Almighty
> has spoken. (Micah 4:4)

Indeed, Schluter and Clements argue that the Old Testament implies
even today that each family should own a plot of land in perpetuity,
with three generations living there together.[24] This suggestion, however, may overlook the change in economic and cultural realities—in
Old Testament times, possession of a piece of land was a guarantee of
income and sustenance, which it is not today. But the text helpfully
points towards kingdom principles, such as the prioritizing of human
need over economic efficiency or the potential for certain goods to be
non-tradable. In a biblical view, homes should not be considered simply as commodities. Accordingly, the law should recognize that people
should be evicted from their houses only as a very final resort, and
during periods of recession, repayment holidays should be mandatory.
A further implication of the biblical value of having property/housing
is that borrowing for investment purposes, as in mortgage borrowing,
is more biblically acceptable than consumer borrowing, "taking the

24. Schluter and Clements (1986), 27–34.

waiting out of wanting." But we have argued that UK housing is over-priced and remains so at the time of writing, thus limiting people's ability to get into the housing market.

One should not, in any case, exaggerate the support in the Bible for property rights. The concepts of Jubilee, the debt Sabbath after seven years, and justice, means that personal property is subordinated to relationship with God. Walter Brueggemann argues that the debt Sabbath noted above, for example, affirms that human society is not based fundamentally "on buying and selling, owning and collecting . . . [P]eople like land cannot be finally owned or managed."[25] Jesus' attitude was finally one of renunciation of property:

> Sell your possessions and give to the poor. Provide purses for yourselves that will not wear out, a treasure in heaven that will not be exhausted, where no thief comes near and no moth destroys. For where your treasure is, there your heart will be also. (Luke 12:33–34)

He is advising followers to eschew economic security and avoid pursuit of wealth—not least in the light of the coming end of the world and judgment after death—while still trusting in God to meet our needs for food, clothing, and shelter:

> So do not worry, saying, "What shall we eat?" or "What shall we drink?" or "What shall we wear?" For the pagans run after all these things, and your heavenly Father knows that you need them. But seek first his kingdom and his righteousness, and all these things will be given to you as well. (Matthew 6:31–33)

An important issue in the context of personal debt is whether the Bible forbids interest (the issue of usury).[26] The word "usury" is based on a Hebrew word meaning to "bite" or "exact" something from someone.[27] Usually, it entails debt in the context of a personal transaction, and not a competitive credit market as economics assumes. The immorality consists in the fact that when the lender has been blessed by God (with sufficient resources to lend money) then he or she is in a position of obligation to offer the same kindness to needy neighbors.

25. Breuggemann (1977), cited in Britton and Sedgwick (2003), 185.

26. Clough et al. (2009).

27. Indeed the Hebrew here, *neshek*, comes from a root meaning "to bite."

Exploitation of the poor by the rich is central, in other words, to the concept of usury.

In the Bible, all interest is generally treated as usurious, unlike modern usage that sees usury as a form of excessive interest. Nehemiah condemns interest exacted from fellow Israelites to pay for grain.

> I pondered them in my mind and then accused the nobles and officials. I told them, "You are exacting usury from your own countrymen!" So I called together a large meeting to deal with them and said: "As far as possible, we have bought back our Jewish brothers who were sold to the Gentiles. Now you are selling your brothers, only for them to be sold back to us!" They kept quiet, because they could find nothing to say. So I continued, "What you are doing is not right. Shouldn't you walk in the fear of our God to avoid the reproach of our Gentile enemies? I and my brothers and my men are also lending the people money and grain. But let the exacting of usury stop! Give back to them immediately their fields, vineyards, olive groves, and houses, and also the usury you are charging them—the hundredth part of the money, grain, new wine, and oil." (Nehemiah 5:7–11)

Leviticus states that interest should not be charged

> if one of your countrymen becomes poor and is unable to support himself among you. (Leviticus 25:35)

The interest is then taking a "bite" from future income, threatening long-term viability of the household of the person in question.[28]

It is widely stated in Scripture that loans to the poor should be at zero interest out of the heart of love that God has for us:[29]

> If you lend money to one of my people among you who is needy, do not be like a moneylender; charge him no interest. (Exodus 22:25)

And God will reward the lender, while he curses the one who charges interest:

28. As an amusing aside, it has been suggested that the word "mortgage" comes originally from the Norman French "mort-gage," meaning death-pledge. In mediaeval English it was used to describe the Faustian pact, made with the devil, in which a man enjoyed a lifetime of power and luxury in exchange for giving the devil his soul!

29. See also Leviticus 25:36–37, "Do not take interest of any kind from him, but fear your God, so that your countryman may continue to live among you. You must not lend him money at interest or sell him food at a profit."

> He who is kind to the poor lends to the Lord, and he will reward him for what he has done. (Proverbs 19:17)

> He who increases his wealth by exorbitant interest amasses it for another, who will be kind to the poor. (Proverbs 28:8)

A parallel to the abuses highlighted in the Bible could be the heavily marketed store cards that demand high interest and often impact most on those on low income. And we have noted above how debts of any kind "bite" into future income, also threatening pensions.

The focus of the above is on loans to the distressed. It is evidently acceptable in the Bible to demand interest for trade with a foreigner, for mutual benefit:

> You may require payment from a foreigner, but you must cancel any debt your brother owes you. (Deuteronomy 15:3)

Banks and money changers were acknowledged in the New Testament, for example by Jesus:

> Well then, you should have put my money on deposit with the bankers, so that when I returned I would have received it back with interest. (Matthew 25:27)

(See chapter 3 above.) In theory, the rule was that money could be borrowed and loaned at interest from a non-Jew, in accordance with the Levitical instruction above. This rule was probably widely flouted; however, in combination with the ban on Christians lending to each other at interest it eventually gave rise to the common profession of moneylending for Jews in medieval Europe. This in turn gave rise to such unhelpful stereotypes as Shakespeare's Shylock and anti-Semitism generally—of course, a gross injustice not least since Jews were in effect "forced" to enter moneylending as one of the few ways they could make a living at that time.

Passages such as that above helped Calvin overturn the medieval ban on interest as long as it was between equals for commercial purposes ("to make concession to the common interest"). But since then, the distinction of lending for commerce or consumption or to rich or poor has been itself blurred in a way Calvin himself might not agree with. Furthermore, bankers remain subject to God's judgment, as discussed in chapter 3 above.

4.3 WAYS FORWARD

As for banking, we consider access to credit essential to household welfare, and the issue is not curtailment of access but whether it can be distributed with less risk of financial distress for households.

The optimization of consumption over the life cycle, as well as the biblical concern for responsibility, restraint, and the avoidance of excessive debt, both seem to suggest a need for limits to be put on household debt. If borrowers cannot be relied upon to be responsible, as the 125 percent loan-to-value (LTV) mortgages eagerly taken on in recent years suggests, then there is an obligation for the lenders or regulators to set prudent limits. This could be via limits on mortgage leverage/gearing such as the LTV ratio, loan to income, or interest payments to income ratios. This is the case in countries such as Germany where it is difficult to obtain a mortgage loan for more than 80 percent of the property value, due to the inability of banks to securitize higher LTV loans as mortgage bonds. In the UK, the FSA set out proposals in 2009 that could entail limits on loan-to-income ratios, although at the time of writing the proposals appear to have been neutered.

If there were such limits on debt, while house prices remain high as in the UK, many more people would stay at home with parents, as in Italy, or would rent. The justice of this could be questioned from a biblical as well as a social perspective. A complementary approach might be, for instance, greater taxation of the housing market to reduce the attractiveness of housing as an investment and thereby reduce house prices. A land tax or a tax on housing services (which did once exist in the UK) would be ways to do this. Or at least, the tax-privileged status of owner occupation could be reconsidered. Another way to achieve this is simply to release planning restrictions further so housing supply could catch up with housing demand, as it does in the US. Falls in house prices would tend to benefit those unable to access the housing ladder, although there would be strident "losers." It is notable that in Germany there has been very little house price inflation in the past decade (although the price of a house is typically high due to exacting building standards).

These arguments are clearly less relevant to the US since house prices tend to adjust more readily in downturns and supply restrictions are less marked than in the UK. Housing supply adjusts rapidly to demand in most parts of the US given freer availability of land. But even there, housing remains a privileged asset (e.g., due to exemption of primary residences from capital gains tax as in the UK) implying prices are higher than they would be without such tax privileges.

Given its greater use by lower income groups, and hence the high default rate it incurs, limitations on the marketing and use of consumer debt may be even more appropriate.[30] After all, it does not provide an asset to pay back the debt and is the most problematic for the poorer members of society. Given the way consumer debt entraps people, it could be seen as akin to the selling of a "birthright" of financial freedom in the future for a worthless meal, as in the story of Jacob and Esau:

> Once when Jacob was cooking some stew, Esau came in from the open country, famished. He said to Jacob, "Quick, let me have some of that red stew! I'm famished!" (That is why he was also called Edom.) Jacob replied, "First sell me your birthright." "Look, I am about to die," Esau said. "What good is the birthright to me?" But Jacob said, "Swear to me first." So he swore an oath to him, selling his birthright to Jacob. Then Jacob gave Esau some bread and some lentil stew. He ate and drank, and then got up and left. So Esau despised his birthright. (Genesis 25:29–34)

Individuals must be responsible for their actions; but the lenders bear as much, if not more, responsibility. The poorest often fall victim to loan sharks charging very high rates and tend to be excluded from cheaper conventional banking. On the other hand, the conventional banks, while excluding the poorest, have spent many millions actively encouraging the buildup of debt, especially amongst other lower income groups, where the greatest margins are to be made. Credit cards sent unsolicited in the mail, or at least unsolicited letters inviting people to apply for a credit card with an attractive introductory interest rate—which would have been unacceptable behavior twenty years ago—is putting people "in the way of temptation" as surely as the serpent did to Eve. And God did not absolve the serpent of blame when he cast Adam and Eve out of Eden. Bank marketing that encourages people to "get it now" is clearly immoral in the same way.

30. These points apply yet more strongly to "Home Credit," the form of high interest doorstep loans used by the poorest members of society.

Such forms of unsecured consumer credit are, in our view, closest to the biblical view of usury. A limit on interest rates chargeable would be one way to reduce consumer debt,[31] since banks would then be much more careful in lending on this basis, the risk premium to cover losses being lower. In this context, the US Credit Card Act of 2009 sought to ensure consumers have sufficient warning of interest rate rises so they could shift their balances. The UK law relating to interest rates was tightened by the Consumer Credit Act 2006, which replaces the extortionate credit bargain test under the Consumer Credit Act 1974 (which was far too favorable to the usurious lender) with that of the unfair creditor/debtor relationship test.

Arguably more could be done, as in France where usury laws setting maximum interest rates still exist. Such limits have a long tradition behind them, as Calvin persuaded the authorities in Geneva to maintain a lawful rate of interest at 5 percent (later $6\frac{2}{3}$ percent), a relatively low rate for that period.[32] Or, alternatively, credit card maxima for borrowing could be related closely to income, while a central credit register could be used to ensure that individuals do not obtain multiple cards and so breach such limits. A third approach would be to limit advertising for consumer credit, thus helping reverse the social perception that it is appropriate to use credit to "have it all and have it now," which the financial industry has been fostering since deregulation in the 1980s.

We note that limits of consumer credit, or even better, a shift in social perceptions towards a more traditional "save first to buy durables" view would have multiple benefits for society in the US and UK. Having realized the benefits of saving to buy goods, individuals would be much more willing and able to save for their own retirement, a tendency that we have seen is being eroded. Household balance sheets resulting would be more like those for households in continental Europe, and would be both more robust to shocks and offer sustainable levels of consumption. However, a major cultural change away

31. Note that this suggestion is distinct from the interest rate controls (Regulation Q) that used to operate in the US till around 1980, which were limits on the interest rate that could be paid on deposits and hence served to limit competition, until they were overtaken by higher inflation and the innovation of money market mutual funds.

32. See Bieler (2005), 147.

from the "retail therapy" and "I deserve it now" self-centered mentality might be difficult to bring about, at least in the short term.

Classical economic theory sees interest as a sine qua non for beneficial economic development. In our view, even from a biblical perspective, the debate on usury should not negatively impact all forms of interest. It would, for example, prohibit safe forms of saving for the relatively badly off and pensioners, leaving them to rely on volatile equity-type products. Nevertheless, non-debt forms of housing finance can be devised and are worthy of consideration. A form of equity loan as employed in Islamic banking could be developed as an alternative to traditional mortgage debt.[33] Sharia-compliant products currently available in the US and UK are based on Ijara, Murabha, and Musharaka methods.[34]

For example, HSBC in the UK offer Musharaka mortgages.[35] In their words:

> [W]e will buy the property jointly with you. The property will be held in trust for both of us by HSBC Trust Company. As you make monthly payments, your share of the property will increase as the bank's share decreases. Assuming you pay a 35% deposit, at the start of the agreement the bank will typically have a 65% share and you will have a 35% share. With each payment you make, you will pay us rent for use of the bank's

33. According to www.islamicmortgages.co.uk, the overarching principle of Islamic finance is that all forms of interest are forbidden. The Islamic financial model works on the basis of risk sharing. The customer and the bank share the risk of any investment on agreed terms and divide any profits between them.

34. Under an Ijara finance plan, the customer chooses the property and agrees a price with the vendor in the normal way. The property is then purchased by the financier, who takes its legal title. The property is then sold onto the customer at the original price, with payment spread over an agreed period of time. During that time, the customer also pays the financier rent for the use of the property. Once the agreed period of time has elapsed, ownership of the property is transferred to the customer. Under a Murabha plan, the customer chooses the property and agrees the price with the vendor in the normal way. Similarly, the financier then purchases the property from the vendor, but on the day of completion it is immediately sold on to the customer at a higher price. The higher price is determined by the value of the property, and the number of years that the financier allows the purchase price to be paid over and the amount of the first payment. The customer then makes regular monthly payments until the purchase price is paid.

35. See http://www.hsbc.co.uk/1/2/personal/travel-international/hsbc-amanah/amanah-home-finance/how-it-works.

share of the property and acquire an additional share for your-self. Once all the payments have been made, you will own all the shares and the property will be transferred to your name on your instruction. You can also make additional lump sum payments that will allow you to acquire additional shares in the property. Your home is at risk if you do not keep up the required payments and comply with the terms of your HSBC Amanah Home Finance plan.

The last point is worth noting. It is not the case that Islamic mortgages are risk free; indeed, they may not even be safer than normal ones, at the same level of gearing. Owing to their complexity they may be costlier. In fact, a problem with much Islamic finance is that it appears to differ little in its fundamentals from more traditional products, i.e., "interest" is theoretically not being charged but the economic effect is equivalent.

Mills cites three other possible means of providing debt-free housing finance;[36] namely partnerships or equity that shares profit and loss, rental contracts where hire charges act as compensation for the owner (Exodus 22:14–15),[37] and leasehold contracts on land (Leviticus 25:14–16, 29–31).[38]

As perspectives from economics and theology both suggest that debt is too high, it raises the issue of whether the current burden of debt can be reduced and if so how—what sort of Jubilee is feasible?[39]

36. Mills (2011).

37. "If a man borrows an animal from his neighbor and it is injured or dies while the owner is not present, he must make restitution. But if the owner is with the animal, the borrower will not have to pay. If the animal was hired, the money paid for the hire covers the loss."

38. "If you sell land to one of your countrymen or buy any from him, do not take advantage of each other. You are to buy from your countryman on the basis of the number of years since the Jubilee. And he is to sell to you on the basis of the number of years left for harvesting crops. When the years are many, you are to increase the price, and when the years are few, you are to decrease the price, because what he is really selling you is the number of crops . . . But if he does not acquire the means to repay him, what he sold will remain in the possession of the buyer until the Year of Jubilee. It will be returned in the Jubilee, and he can then go back to his property. If a man sells a house in a walled city, he retains the right of redemption a full year after its sale. During that time he may redeem it. If it is not redeemed before a full year has passed, the house in the walled city shall belong permanently to the buyer and his descendants. It is not to be returned in the Jubilee."

39. Ferguson (2008).

Unfortunately those options that are feasible would cause major losses to others in the community:

- Historically, debt has often been "monetized," meaning that central banks and governments have eased monetary policy and generated inflation. Such inflation would drive up wages as debt falls in real terms, giving a "Jubilee" effect, but this would tend to inflict losses on savers, who may be pensioners reliant on their interest income. There is some suspicion at the time of writing that central banks have become "soft on inflation" to ease the adjustment of balance sheets, notably via the policy of low interest rates and "quantitative easing," albeit also seeking to prevent even more damaging deflation.[40]

- Meanwhile, if commercial banks were simply to forgive debts as a "Jubilee" and became bankrupt as a result, the losses would either again be inflicted on depositors, or more likely on the public debt, as discussed in chapter 5 below—and thus largely impact future generations.

The church has a clear role to play as offering an alterative culture to that of a life based on debt and consumption. Given the way individuals seem to misjudge even their own best economic interests, this would be of general benefit. For example, the church could help facilitate a shift in social perceptions towards a more traditional "save first to buy durables" view, as emphasized in the Bible texts cited in section 4.2 above.

Meanwhile, Christian churches need to be visible communities that help their members, akin to the early church of Acts wherein:

> All the believers were together and had everything in common. Selling their possessions and goods, they gave to anyone as he had need. (Acts 2:44–45)

They were thus an example to the rest of society. Jesus also said:

> Give to the one who asks you, and do not turn away from the one who wants to borrow from you. (Matthew 5:42)

---

40. As noted by Mills (2011), deflation becomes of major concern precisely in the context of money-fixed debt contracts, whose real burden increases when general prices fall.

Individual Christians need to feel accountable and available to one another, and support one another against poverty arising from debt.

There is also a question of spending priorities for the church, with more being made available for the poor and less for, say, opulent buildings; and avoidance of substantial ongoing debt for building projects. The church is unable to insist on governments legislating against domestic poverty unless it can demonstrate practical examples of acting as salt and light:

> You are the salt of the earth. But if the salt loses its saltiness, how can it be made salty again? It is no longer good for anything, except to be thrown out and trampled by men. You are the light of the world. A city on a hill cannot be hidden. Neither do people light a lamp and put it under a bowl. Instead they put it on its stand, and it gives light to everyone in the house. In the same way, let your light shine before men, that they may see your good deeds and praise your Father in heaven. (Matthew 5:13–16)

Again, whereas the economic paradigm implies that consumption is always good, recent experience has shown its risks if pursued to excess, and Scripture cautions against giving it too much prominence in our lives. Churches need to preach on this matter. Consumerism— defined by Gregg as "attaching too much significance to material goods, even to the extent of defining ourselves by the number and type of our possessions, and measuring our worth in terms of what we have compared to others"[41]—is a key challenge for Christians as well as for society as a whole.

Western culture as a whole, including many Christians, have lost the kingdom virtue of temperance, which "moderates the attraction of pleasures and provides balance in the use of created goods."[42] This means Christians need to assess whether they have been absorbed by the consumer society without taking note, in particular, of whether they are borrowing responsibly or not. Temperance needs to be proclaimed from the pulpit. The church should also critique the social pressures that induced over-indebtedness, assessing whether banks— and the government via student loans—create a form of structural evil, a social norm that people feel induced to go heavily into debt.

41. Gregg (2010).
42. Nichols (2008).

People need to take advice before borrowing when the human tendency is to be too proud to seek help, or too stubborn once our mind is made up:

> When pride comes, then comes disgrace, but with humility
> comes wisdom. (Proverbs 11:2)

The church should also be encouraging and resourcing financial education with an ethical basis, such as the UK's Christians Against Poverty (CAP) Money Course, which teaches avoidance of debt and use of cash as a means of restraint in expenditure.[43] There is a need for teaching discernment in debt and consumption decisions.

And finally the church must model the virtue of mercy, of caring for those who have suffered misfortune due to debts, unemployment, or other consequences of the crisis. One aspect is debt counseling within the church or by charities linked to churches, such as CAP in the UK, who provide such counseling and debt management free of charge while the churches give pastoral support. Christians can be encouraged to provide finance to one another, within families and congregations, to avoid debt.[44] Church-based credit unions could be set up to encourage responsible use of debt. But more generally Christians must show mercy by pastoral, personal, and financial support for those who are now weak and vulnerable owing to debt problems, as Jesus himself urged:

> Blessed are the merciful, for they will be shown mercy.
> (Matthew 5:7)

43. See www.capuk.org
44. Mills (2009).

Chapter 5

The Government Sector—
Public Debt

5.1 FROM AN ECONOMICS PERSPECTIVE

Government debt needs to be issued when there is an imbalance between government revenue and expenditure, regardless of the size of the public sector. Nevertheless, background to the economic controversy about public debt is the conflict between what may be called the "free market" economic approach and the "social market," a conflict whose primary focus is the overall size of government. The difference hinges largely on whether there should be laissez-faire policies or whether there should be benefit-based "safety nets" for those facing difficulties in life. The free market approach argues for a small public sector, focused on areas such as police, justice, and defense (the "minimal state"), while the social market emphasizes social security, pensions, and public health care.

As noted in chapter 2, a pure utilitarian approach to economics and economic policy often leads to a preference for the free market approach, while inclusion of some wider political element such as a social contract may tend to encourage the social market approach. In practice, the minimal state remains a theoretical construct, but the tension remains between, on the one hand, the US and Japan, which have relatively small public sectors, and, on the other, most

EU countries with relatively large ones. The view taken of laissez-faire affects views both of the size of government *per se* (i.e., what share of GDP should be taken up in taxation and government expenditure), and the degree to which the economy is seen as self-righting in response to shocks. The free market approach tends to suggest that the economy will recover and discretionary deficits and debts are not needed, while the social market approach tends to emphasize government spending rises to help the economy out of recession.

On the social market view, fiscal deficits can be seen as an optimal response to cyclical weakness, buoying the economy when demand falls. And this is what has happened in the current downturn. To some extent, this will take place via the operation of automatic stabilizers, which entail a decline in tax revenue and a rise in benefit payments when there is a downturn. But governments may also carry out discretionary fiscal boosts such as public investment programs to further buoy the economy. All such deficits will generate rises in public debt, which is typically in the form of bonds to be repaid in the future.

In the current downturn there has also been quantitative easing by central banks, notably in the US and UK, which entails, in effect, governments printing money. This probably helped support economic activity, but it also poses a risk of future inflation. Certainly, if inflation were generated this would be consistent with behavior over the past half century when governments, in effect, expropriated bond holders by high inflation, which massively reduced the real value of bonds. The inflation of the 1970s in particular inflicted catastrophic losses on holders of government bonds. There is a clear incentive for governments to undertake this again, which may be increased by the partial use of money financing, although the independence of the central banks in the US and UK should reduce this risk.

There are arguments as to whether fiscal deficits, especially if bond-financed, will actually have an impact on aggregate demand, or whether households and firms will reduce their consumption and investment to allow for future taxes to repay debt. Such effects may depend on how much confidence the public have in the government's ability to stabilize the economy. An additional offset to the ability of deficits to generate a recovery may arise if rising public debt induces higher long-term interest rates since this discourages business investment in particular. Such rises in interest rates may be particularly likely when foreign parties are the main holders of debt or when holders fear that the government will generate inflation to avoid its debt burden.

A broader issue that arises for poorer countries is the risk of incurring unsustainable foreign currency debts to the international capital markets and rich country governments as a counterpart to government deficits. Capital inflows to poor countries have often been subject to "sudden stops" when doubt arises among creditors about solvency, as in Latin America in 1982 and East Asia in 1997. The adverse consequences for economic activity of such "sudden stops" are worsened if expenditure has been unproductive owing to corruption. The experience of EU countries such as Greece, Portugal, and Ireland since 2009 shows that even advanced countries are not immune to "sudden stops" in capital flows and hence there is no cause for complacency in the US or UK.

Economists distinguish between cyclical and structural fiscal deficits, where the latter are persistent even when the economy attains its normal or "trend" rate of growth. Structural deficits threaten continual rises in public debt, and these are of particular concern given the oncoming challenge to public finances of population ageing. The US and UK governments have been widely accused by economists of running structural deficits in the boom period up to 2007, meaning that the fiscal position was weaker than that which is consistent with balanced budget over the cycle. The data underlying the the Organization for Economic Co-operation and Development (OECD) Economic Outlook for May 2011 shows that both countries ran structural deficits averaging 3.8–3.9 percent of GDP over 2002–7. In the US this related to tax cuts, in the UK it was more a matter of excessive growth of expenditures. Both governments tended to overestimate the sustainability of tax revenues arising from the financial sector and financing activity in the boom years.

Structural deficits in the boom, in turn, may have made economic growth and the credit/house price bubble larger. In the UK at least, it can be argued that this was a consequence of the desire of the government to have rapid spending growth for electoral reasons, without raising the necessary taxation; in the US perhaps it was more an ideological view that low taxes benefit the economy. In both cases, there are clear parallels with the household sector's desire to consume beyond its means by borrowing. Given the limited amount of saving in both the US and the UK, both government and households ended up borrowing from foreigners, directly or via the banks. The US debt to China, which holds a significant proportion of Treasury securities, is one example of this.

Fiscal policy has a specific role to play in a banking crisis, in that there is typically recapitalization of failing banks, which entails a steep rise in the level of public debt, as discussed in chapters 1 and 3. This has been a major component in the rise in public sector debt since 2007. But the depth of the recession also led to major rises in public debt due to automatic and discretionary fiscal easing.

Economists in most advanced countries concur that cuts in public spending and rises in taxation are needed in coming years to balance the government's books in the context of massive growth in debt and slow overall economic growth. Failure to do so could threaten a "flight" by external creditors and a possible fiscal crisis along the lines of that being suffered by Greece, Portugal, and Ireland at the time of writing. That said, there remain differences on how quickly to undertake fiscal consolidation, which links to beliefs about the relationship of deficits to economic growth. At the time of writing, the US and UK are at opposite ends of the spectrum, with the UK undertaking aggressive consolidation and the US being slow to adopt a consolidation plan, partly due to political disagreements—and risking thereby higher levels of long-term debt.

5.2 FROM A THEOLOGICAL PERSPECTIVE

The New Testament contends that the state and government should in general be supported by citizens as instituted by God to be a source of stability (including economic stability), being "God's servant to do you good."

> Everyone must submit himself to the governing authorities, for there is no authority except that which God has established. The authorities that exist have been established by God. Consequently, he who rebels against the authority is rebelling against what God has instituted, and those who do so will bring judgment on themselves. For rulers hold no terror for those who do right, but for those who do wrong. Do you want to be free from fear of the one in authority? Then do what is right and he will commend you. For he is God's servant to do you good.

But if you do wrong, be afraid, for he does not bear the sword for nothing. He is God's servant, an agent of wrath to bring punishment on the wrongdoer. Therefore, it is necessary to submit to the authorities, not only because of possible punishment but also because of conscience. (Romans 13:1–5)

Also payment of taxes is an obligation, as Paul goes on to say in Romans:

This is also why you pay taxes, for the authorities are God's servants, who give their full time to governing. Give everyone what you owe him: If you owe taxes, pay taxes; if revenue, then revenue; if respect, then respect; if honor, then honor. (Romans 13:6–7)

Jesus states the same in Matthew's Gospel. Referring to a coin with Caesar's head on it he says:

Give to Caesar what is Caesar's, and to God what is God's. (Matthew 22:21)

There are theological arguments to help the poor—including those affected by debt problems—that can be applied not only to individuals but also at the level of government, and are considered by many to support a "social market" approach to fiscal policy. For example, the tithe in its original Old Testament usage can be seen in part as a form of taxation: in Deuteronomy the tithe is to be used for a religious celebration two years out of three, but in the third year it is to be set aside to provide for the Levites—who functioned as civil servants as well as priests—and for "immigrants, orphans, and widows."

Be sure to set aside a tenth of all that your fields produce each year. Eat the tithe of your grain, new wine, and oil, and the first-born of your herds and flocks in the presence of the Lord your God at the place he will choose as a dwelling for his Name, so that you may learn to revere the Lord your God always. But if that place is too distant and you have been blessed by the Lord your God and cannot carry your tithe (because the place where the Lord will choose to put his Name is so far away), then exchange your tithe for silver, and take the silver with you and go to the place the Lord your God will choose. Use the silver to buy whatever you like: cattle, sheep, wine or other fermented drink, or anything you wish. Then you and your household shall eat there in the presence of the Lord your God and rejoice. And do not neglect the Levites living in your towns, for they have no allotment or inheritance of their own. At the end of every three years, bring all the tithes of that year's produce and store it in your towns, so that the Levites (who have no allotment or inheritance of their own) *and the aliens, the fatherless, and the widows* who live in your towns may come and eat and be satisfied, and so that the Lord your God may bless you in all the work of your hands. (Deuteronomy 14:22–29; emphasis added)

Indeed, rulers are held responsible for injustice to the poor.

A ruler who oppresses the poor is like a driving rain that leaves no crops. (Proverbs 28:3)

The servant in Isaiah—identified as, among other things, the nation of Israel, Christ himself, and his church—is called to bring "justice to the nations" (Isaiah 42:1). This could be seen as consistent with Romans 13:1–7 if the pursuit of justice includes justice to the poor. Such passages are widely considered to imply that a basic welfare system and progressive taxation are biblically based ideas, providing a form of structural justice in society.

As regards borrowing, a state in a surplus position is blessed by God, notably if debt is foreign. Deuteronomy, for example, states that:

The Lord your God will bless you as he has promised, and you will lend to many nations but will borrow from none. You will rule over many nations but none will rule over you. (Deuteronomy 15:6)[1]

The implication is that the surplus nation has a whip hand over the debtor, as has been the case for developing country debt and is becoming the case for advanced countries with very high levels of public debt. As for households, the nation-state that is a borrower is the "servant of the lender" and has reduced scope for flexibility, for example, in providing famine relief, development aid, or pursuing "just wars." The East Asian countries and notably China are the creditors of countries such as the US and the UK and this could yet translate into greater political influence and shifts in the balance of power. Bear in mind again the proverb:

1. See also Deuteronomy 28:12: "The Lord will open the heavens, the storehouse of his bounty, to send rain on your land in season and to bless all the work of your hands. You will lend to many nations but will borrow from none."

The borrower is servant to the lender. (Proverbs 22:7)

This insight can apply to some extent at a national as well as at an individual level.[2]

The arguments above favor a public sector that seeks to correct some of the grosser inequalities in income and life chances that would be generated by the free market. But it need not imply a need to run deficits on average over the cycle. Rather, biblical prudence as set out above would suggest the aim of balancing the books over the cycle, while running deficits for stabilization purposes during recessions. The profligacy of governments running structural deficits could be compared to those rulers criticized for their extravagance in the Bible. Jeremiah, for example, wrote:

> He [the King of Judah] says, "I will build myself a great palace with spacious upper rooms." So he makes large windows in it, panels it with cedar, and decorates it in red. Does it make you a king to have more and more cedar? (Jeremiah 22:14–15)

A downside of the current growth in public debt is that future generations of taxpayers will be obliged to finance what can be seen as errors by current government, bankers, and borrowers, and hence our children will have to repay debts we incur. This situation is redolent of the traditional curse that Jeremiah quotes:

> The fathers have eaten sour grapes, and the children's teeth are set on edge. (Jeremiah 31:29)

This is not seen as God's desire, however. Rather, the Bible speaks of intergenerational fairness. Jeremiah again:

> Instead, everyone will die for his own sin; whoever eats sour grapes—his own teeth will be set on edge. (Jeremiah 31:30)

This suggests that it is not God's will that punishment should continue down the generations, and similarly we should not place burdens

---

2. The difference between a nation-state and an individual or firm is that a nation-state can default on its debts without bankruptcy, as was memorably shown in the Latin American debt crisis of 1982. That said, the path of default is not an easy one, not least because countries find themselves cut off from global finance and typically have to undergo wrenching fiscal adjustments in order to "live within their means" without the boost from external capital inflows.

on future generations that we did not have to bear.[3] Equally, intergenerational fairness could be seen as contrary to Jesus' golden rule:

> Do to others what you would have them do to you. (Matthew 7:12)

The coming generation, likely to be burdened with fiscal debts, has also suffered from the rise in land prices, as well as adverse conditions in student finance. In the UK, the "fathers" benefited from university grants but today's "children" have to incur massive debts to gain a university education, while in the US student fees are far higher in real terms than they were for the previous generation. The coming generation will also have to finance future pensions against an adverse demographic background, with the large baby boom cohort now approaching retirement.

Alternatively, if lenders to the government are expropriated by inflation, then this may be regarded as akin to false weights and measures that the prophets repeatedly condemned, as does the law of Moses:

> Shall I acquit a man with dishonest scales, with a bag of false weights? (Micah 6:11)

> Use honest scales and honest weights, an honest *ephah* and an honest *hin*. I am the Lord your God, who brought you out of Egypt. (Leviticus 19:36)

5.3 WAYS FORWARD

Is current US and UK fiscal policy placing too much of a burden on future generations? It can be argued that the rescue of the economy from the crisis was warranted, but the long-term burden also links to how loose fiscal policy was as we went into the crisis. From OECD figures quoted in the section above, as well as estimates from other respected institutions, there would appear to have been major structural deficits during the boom. This, in turn, means that the overall deficit in the recession is much larger and more difficult to remove than would otherwise be the case—and the debt buildup much greater. Underlying

3. There is a similar message in Ezekiel 18:1–3, "The word of the Lord came to me: 'What do you people mean by quoting this proverb about the land of Israel: "The fathers eat sour grapes, and the children's teeth are set on edge"? As surely as I live,' declares the Sovereign Lord, 'you will no longer quote this proverb in Israel.'"

the structural deficits was a willingness of governments, for electoral reasons, not to levy sufficient tax to fully finance the level of public expenditure that they chose to offer. This is economically destabilizing and contrary to the biblical injunction for the state to promote stability and justice. Equally to be criticized is any future realization of the risk that the government debt will be "monetized"—eroded by inflation—which would have major redistributive consequences.

We contend that governments misled their populations by the earlier fiscal policies of structural deficit in the boom years. By boosting growth, it made people more willing to go into debt, by leading them to believe their income growth and house price appreciation would continue to be high. This was aggravated by over-optimistic statements, for example, by the UK government who claimed that sustainable growth in GDP was as much as 2.75 percent per annum when respected independent forecasters considered it to be 2.4 percent even before the crisis.[4] The difference is very significant over the long term and meant businesses as well as individuals were not correctly informed about the long-term risks of their balance sheet positions.

There are similar criticisms to be made in the short term. Quite apart from evidence from crises in other countries, UK experience of 1974 and 1991, and that of the US in the 1980s and early 1990s showed that *credit-driven booms*, like the one clearly underway up to 2007, *are only temporary and the subsequent downturns highly destructive.* Accordingly, governments had a responsibility to warn the population as well as adjusting fiscal, monetary, and regulatory policy to deflate the boom. To do otherwise would be like the false prophets of Jeremiah, who proclaimed:

"Peace, peace," when there is no peace. (Jeremiah 8:10–11)

In fact, in the UK the former Chancellor unrealistically proclaimed an end to "boom and bust." Governments seem to have sought to create the illusion that the economy can be run on a "no-risk" basis, which helped generate the profligate behavior of bankers and households highlighted in chapters 3 and 4. In effect, such a belief led people to feel insulated from the consequences of poor decisions and bad investments.

4. Such as the National Institute of Economic and Social Research.

In more detail, it can be argued that governments should have warned that growth was above trend due to structural deficits, and hence future income projections should be conservative. Also, they should have warned that when the bulk of the population has become fully geared (i.e., having debt service obligations that left no disposable income after ongoing needs), the growth of personal debt and hence consumption would stall. There is initially a sharp correction (as we see today in the US and UK) as those people who have jobs try to rebuild their balance sheets, while those losing their jobs may default, and private demand actually falls. Stock prices and house prices both fall as a consequence, which aggravates the downturn and increases related defaults. Even in the medium term, consumption can for some time be expected to revert to the level of the status quo before financial liberalization in the early 1970s, when consumption rose as fast as average earnings and no faster.

Future governments must therefore be more ready to warn about this cycle, as well as avoiding fiscal laxity. Mills suggested an independent fiscal commission could be appointed to ensure that governments run responsible fiscal policies, and recent UK moves to establish an Office of Budgetary Responsibility have moved in this direction.[5] Equally, the establishment of the US Financial Stability Oversight Council and the Financial Policy Committee in the UK have created bodies with responsibilities for warning and acting on the dangers of financial crisis arising from future credit-driven booms.

In assessing fiscal policy, it can also be asked whether the tax system promotes the type of private debt highlighted as a problem in chapter 4. Certainly this is the case for corporations where interest on debt is tax deductible while dividends on equity is not. This tax bias has contributed to the rise in corporate debt and arguably led the level of bankruptcy to be higher than it would otherwise be. In the US there remain provisions for tax deductibility of mortgage interest, which was abolished in the UK some time ago. This provision will tend to boost indebtedness in the US. In both countries, it can be argued that the low level of taxation of owner-occupied housing has contributed to the high level of house prices, and hence of mortgage debt. Hence there is a need to reconsider some of these tax provisions.

5. Mills (2009).

In this context, we also argue that the student debt necessary to attend college in the US and as increasingly mandated by government in the UK is conditioning people to expect to be in debt for all their lives, weakening their resistance to credit cards, excessive mortgages, etc. Two alternative means of financing university education that do not involve debt are a "graduate tax," as used in Australia, and simply providing tertiary education free as a public good, as is the case for primary and secondary education.[6]

The rescue of banks in 2008 was evidently necessary, but there is a need for governments to reshape regulation so that such "rescues" are not needed again. Following the point made above, the safety net that protects banks from liquidity and (in some cases) solvency problems also led bankers to feel insulated from the consequences of poor decisions and bad investments. The difficulty is that a "safety net" can easily lead to complacency and risky behavior, an issue of moral hazard as highlighted in chapter 3. But a lack of a safety net would expose the economy to extreme risks. The generosity of the current approach could store up greater risks for the future. Hence, the current proposals for higher capital, separation of retail banking from wholesale banking, and "living wills" to facilitate winding up of banks in case they get into difficulties. Regulation may not be the sole answer, as suggested in chapter 3, section 3—one response in line with justice considerations is that there should be no "free pardon" or "golden farewell" for bankers whose institutions have failed and who prove to be directly culpable.

Like banks, the public cannot treat the government as autonomous and omnipotent; this is akin to a form of idolatry. Rather, we all have the responsibility to understand and ask questions on these issues, to take a view and press for it in public and via Congressmen and MPs. And to stand up for truth, calling our leaders to account when we discover we are being misled.

---

6. An objection to the "graduate tax" is that emigrants can avoid the tax (although emigrants may also default on student debt). The objection to free tertiary education is that it entails a transfer from (poorer) taxpayers to richer individuals who benefit financially from a university education.

Chapter 6

Conclusions and Recommendations

Focusing on experience of both the US and the UK, we have highlighted three long-term issues from the financial crisis, namely the role of banks in provoking the crisis, the burden of debt on households, and the debt of the public sector. Biblical theology has important lessons to teach us in all these areas where there is now a prevailing "conventional" wisdom from economics. The combination of insights from economics and biblical theology helps us approach policy and address personal behavior from a new and more radical kingdom viewpoint based on wider considerations such as values and virtues.

We have seen a number of themes emerging. In particular, we see that various actors in the economy—the banks, many households, and the government—have acted in recent years to maximize their personal benefit in the pursuit of self-interest. This is precisely as economic theory predicts. Bankers were seeking higher remuneration, households more consumption, and governments to be popular. But there were flaws in the rationality of each of these approaches, contrary to the expectations of economic theory but strongly in line with the biblical view of the fall and humankind's imperfection and weakness. Underlying this, we see common aspects of greed, selfishness, and the impatience of many individuals in all three aspects of the crisis.[1]

1. It is ironic that the riots that shook the UK in early August 2011 had some of

These aspects were not only undesirable in themselves but also often counterproductive. Bankers put their livelihoods at risk by their self-interested actions, since their institutions risked insolvency. Households went to such extremes of indebtedness that they risked default, bankruptcy, and repossession in the short run, and impoverished old age in the longer term. By doing so, they fed bankers' self-interest further. We contend that in the boom governments effectively misled their populations about sustainable economic growth, also "doping" the economy with loose fiscal policy and giving the impression that risk had been abolished, in the economic realm as in others. Ultimately, in search of (continued) power, they consequently encouraged both bankers and households to believe that high levels of debt could be sustainable, leading to catastrophe for many.

For there have been major casualties of this process. These include not only bankers out of work and households who regret the debts they have incurred, but also "innocent bystanders" such as those unemployed due to the recession (despite their industry being uninvolved in the "bubble"), unpaid creditors of those going bankrupt, depositors suffering lower interest rates as banks recapitalize, and those affected in developing countries. Casualties also include the coming generation, who are already charged highly for higher education, who (in the UK at least) are now also priced out of housing, and who will be burdened with future taxes and pensions bills to pay off and sustain government debt. There is strong evidence of injustice in a number of these consequences. The US and UK governments have little choice but to impose far-reaching fiscal austerity programs on already burdened nations—a challenge that has been accepted in the UK but, at the time of writing, not in the US.

We have highlighted some potential remedies in line with the kingdom of God that Scripture consistently highlights. We agree that tighter conventional bank regulation is part of the answer, as is currently being implemented by governments—including regulation of

---

the same features, albeit with the important difference that people broke the law. Nevertheless, we saw individuals seeking "instant gratification" by pillaging shops of desirable consumer goods (TVs, iPads, mobile phones, top end bicycles). They again showed greed, selfishness, and impatience, and many have ended up damaging their life chances by gaining criminal records. Two other recent examples of this syndrome are the falsification of expenses by UK Members of Parliament and the illegal hacking of mobile phones by newspaper journalists.

bonus schemes. But we contend that a wider focus on *values* and encouragement of *virtues* in banking, as well as a reestablishment of the importance of *relationships* between borrowers and lenders is needed to truly generate a stable and socially beneficial financial system. Equally, while some limits on household debt seem justified, the underlying social pressure for ever-more consumption—the idea that "a man's life consists of the abundance of his possessions"—needs to be tempered where possible. This is not only in the interests of those concerned but is desirable due to environmental aspects also. And governments need to recognize the benefits of restraining public spending on average over the cycle to be in line with tax revenue.

A biblical analysis of the current situation implies that idolatry —be it of banks as institutions, of governments as providers, and of money and wealth more generally—needs to be recognized and the structural injustices and evils such idolatry generates need to be condemned. Besides the obvious points, this includes a call for greater individual responsibility to be accepted so that people no longer hide behind "institutions." If they can find a voice, churches can play a helpful role in these necessary cultural transformations, as well as standing ready to critique governments when they act contrary to truth or justice, and offering merciful support to casualties of the recession.

In outlining a biblical approach we have, in effect, undertaken a critique of the overall aims of individuals as assumed by economics —wealth, consumption, power—in contrast to Jesus' proclamation of the kingdom of God, the law of love for God and neighbor, and responsible stewardship of resources. With the aims of "rational economic humanity" having been taken largely on board by policymakers, there is a need to energetically broadcast and urge the benefits of the alternative biblical approach.

We contend that a number of recommendations for governments, households, the church, banks, and for further research emerge from the confrontation of economics and theology that we have undertaken. These as follows:

Broad recommendations:

- The dominance of economics as the ruling paradigm of society needs to be challenged, and the impact of its amoral approach on the way we live counteracted.

- Stewardship of resources, mutually beneficial relationships, and foresight need to be restored at the heart of the economy and society, to replace the greed, selfishness, and impatience exhibited in the crisis.

- Everyone must consider why we treat the government and its policies as something sacrosanct, rather than the responsibility of us all; and why bankers sought to avoid personal responsibility for the fate of their institutions, again by viewing them as unchallengeable entities.

- The scope of personal indebtedness must be limited through government regulation as well as improved bank behavior and individual restraint.

Recommendations to governments:

- Governments have a responsibility to warn of the consequences of a credit and housing boom, and act to defuse such booms.

- The degree to which the tax system, and other aspects of government policy, promote indebtedness must be counteracted.

- Notably in the UK, the government needs to consider how house prices can be reduced relative to incomes, given the injustice current levels present to those excluded from the market.

- The size and influence of the financial sector *vis-à-vis* the wider economy, and its vulnerability to crisis, should be reduced.

- Fiscal policy must avoid "structural" deficits persisting over the cycle, which may boost growth but potentially mislead the population about sustainable levels of expenditure and debt.

Recommendations to banks and businesses:

- To accept tighter regulation but also to realize it is not sufficient to generate a stable banking system; values must be adhered to and virtues encouraged both among employees and top managers.

- Responsibility must be taken by lenders for financial distress incurred through imprudent extension of consumer credit.

- The centrality of relationships must be reestablished in lending and other financial transactions.

- Experienced staff should be retained in banks to provide stability and "institutional memory" of past crises.

Recommendations to the church:

- That Christians be encouraged to engage in the financial sector and pursue careers in business and banking.

- The church should urge the merits of an alternative culture to unbridled debt and consumerism.

- The church should offer debt counseling, relief of poverty generated by debt, and financial education, including promotion of a "save first" approach to purchase of durables, property and also to retirement.

Areas for further research:

- Is there a way that existing burdens of household debt can be reduced? Is a "Jubilee" with widespread debt forgiveness feasible or desirable?

- Are non-credit forms of housing finance superior to interest-based ones?

- Study of the lending practices of continental European countries where credit is less freely available and saving more common than in the US and UK.

- Consideration of the impact on future generations of recent fiscal policy, and subsequent burden of public debt and pensions, as well as the level of house prices and the burden of student debt.[2]

---

2. Morisy (2011) provides an interesting Christian analysis of the issue of intergenerational equity, with a central challenge to baby boomers to value the rights of tomorrow alongside those of today, and to extend justice into the future, behaving generously and imaginatively.

Generic Aspects of Financial Instability and the Financial Crisis

As outlined in Davis and Karim, financial crises like the one that began in 2007 are not random events but share key common features.[1] As highlighted in Table 1, the process often starts with a favorable shock to the economy and financial system that boosts growth and investment. But in some circumstances, this can lead to a buildup of vulnerability in the economy and financial system, associated with overextension of balance sheets and buildup of financial imbalances. Price-based measures of asset values rise and price-based measures of risk fall. Balance sheets grow, short-term funding increases, and leverage rises. These exacerbate the boom and lead to a crisis when a secondary (adverse) shock hits a vulnerable financial system.

The crisis that then ensues features liquidity problems for financial institutions (provoked by credit risk or market risk) as discussed in chapter 1. In turn, there is further propagation in a crisis period (systemic risk) that typically entails policy reactions if the crisis is sufficiently severe, and considerable adverse economic consequences (what we can term the "costs of instability").

---

1. Davis and Karim (2009).

Table 1: Generic Aspects of Financial Instability

Phase of Crisis	Nature	Example of Features
Primary (favorable) shock	Diverse	Deregulation, monetary or fiscal easing, invention, change in market sentiment
Propagation—buildup of vulnerability	Common—main subject of macroprudential surveillance	New entry to financial markets, debt accumulation, asset price booms, innovation in financial markets, underpricing of risk, risk concentration, lower capital adequacy for banks, unsustainable macro policy
Secondary (adverse) shock	Diverse	Monetary, fiscal or regulatory tightening, asymmetric trade shock
Propagation—crisis	Common	Failure of institution or market leading to systemic risk, i.e., failure of other institutions owing to direct links, uncertainty in presence of asymmetric information or generalized failure due to common shock
Policy action	Common—main subject of crisis resolution	Deposit insurance, lender of last resort, general monetary and fiscal easing
Economic consequences	Common—scope depends on severity and policy action	Credit rationing and wider uncertainty leading to fall in GDP, notably investment, which may also impact on economic growth in the long run

This approach can readily be applied to the sub-prime crisis as described in chapter 1. As regards favorable shocks, the monetary policy stance of most countries was relaxed from 2001 onwards, as policy sought to stimulate growth in the wake of the equity bear market in the absence of significant inflationary pressures. Underlying this was the additional shift of globalization and the growth of China, the low price of whose goods helped to keep inflation low. There was clearly an easing of entry conditions to financial markets, leading to heightened competition and risk taking. Easy financing of hedge funds is one example; another is the growth of bank subsidiaries such as SIVs and conduits to hold securitized assets, an innovation that facilitated entry of new institutions to the market. Furthermore, origination of lending to US sub-prime households was often by non-banks not previously active in that market.

As regards debt accumulation and asset price booms, generating vulnerable balance sheets in the financial and nonfinancial sectors; we saw rises in debt of both the corporate and household sectors in the US and much of Europe over the mid-2000s, with prices of equities and real estate rising alongside. These were, as noted, potentially unsustainable and the more recent fall in asset prices combined with high debt has led to weak balance sheets and widespread defaults and insolvency. Innovation in financial markets, which increases uncertainty during a crisis, was a key aspect of the sub-prime crisis. All financial innovations give rise to a risk of financial instability because their behavior in a period of turbulence is unknown. The innovation of structured products such as ABS was, by its nature, likely to generate such uncertainty in extreme form given the opacity and difficulty of pricing the instruments even in good times. Despite this, they benefited from a liquidity premium as securities, while investors were apparently unconcerned with the principal-agent problems and information gaps that are fundamental to that innovation.

Risk concentration and lower capital adequacy for banks, which reduces robustness to shocks is the final indicator. Banks' risk-adjusted capital ratios seemed sound in 2007, but the conduits and SIVs generated hidden difficulties for banks, as did "warehousing risk" arising from failure to dispose of loans by securitization in a manner expected. Highly rated ABS were overpriced because banks and markets were unaware of the risks they posed. In terms of a negative shock, monetary tightening was indeed on the cards in 2007 owing to shrinking output gaps and higher energy prices, although it is harder to suggest that this feature actually triggered the crisis. And the authorities have indeed been forced to intervene massively with public money to prevent the banking system from collapsing, by recapitalizing banks and guaranteeing loans and deposits. The impact of the crisis on economic growth and employment has been severe.

Appendix 2

Why Banks Are Fragile and Need Regulation

In the main text we frequently mention bank runs, solvency, or liquidity problems as well as banking regulation. This Appendix seeks to assist in understanding the nature and causes of such events. A simple stylized illustration of bank balance sheets "before" and "after" recent structural changes in the industry helps one understand both the underlying fragility of banks and the consequent need for regulation, as well as the evolution of banks' activities in recent years.[2] Consider first Figure 1, which shows the balance sheet of a "traditional" bank, such as a small savings bank or building society. Assets are liquid assets and illiquid loans, while liabilities are retail deposits. The difference between assets and liabilities is the bank's capital.

The key feature of banks that leads to fragility is the mismatch in maturity of assets and liabilities. Because customers usually only require withdrawal of funds on a random basis, the bank can survive with low levels of liquid assets (cash, short-term government bonds) and invest other monies in higher yielding but illiquid long-term loans, while providing "liquidity insurance"—the promise of full redemption—to deposit clients at all times.[3]

2. The author has used this analysis in a number of talks in churches and to men's groups.

3. Diamond and Dybvig (1983).

However, if the depositors consider that banks may be unable to pay them back, there can be a "run" when all depositors require funds at once. In this liquidity problem, which rapidly exhausts liquid assets, the bank is then unable to sell its illiquid assets for full value (due to asymmetric information—the so-called "fire sale" problem) and becomes insolvent. A bank can, of course, also become insolvent due to simple losses on assets in excess of capital (as for the Dunfermline Building Society). Then, bank runs can become contagious across the system if customers consider other banks to have similar balance sheet weaknesses (which cannot be detected precisely due to asymmetric information) and/or counterparty links to the failing bank.

Figure 1: "Traditional" Bank

Assets	Liabilities
Liquid assets	Capital
	Retail deposits
Illiquid loans	

Bank regulation is a way to reduce risks in this simple framework. Capital adequacy regulation ensures that the level of capital is sufficient to cover unexpected losses due to loan defaults in a downturn, while appropriate pricing of loans should cover expected losses. Liquidity regulation seeks to ensure that liquidity can be accessed sufficient to cover peak demands for deposit withdrawals. And when liquid assets are inadequate, the central bank (as lender of last resort) can provide liquidity to the bank, at its discretion, so as to meet demands for redemption. Deposit insurance, usually run by Ministries of Finance, seeks to prevent runs from occurring by giving depositors a guarantee of the nominal value of their assets.

The key changes to this framework that are relevant to developments in recent years are, first, deregulation that has typically removed previous limits to competition between banks, and hence put greater weight on the remaining prudential regulations. In the UK, for example, deregulation entailed the entry of banks to the mortgage market, growth of investment banking activities by commercial banks, and scope for building societies such as Northern Rock to demutualize and become banks. In the US there was, for example, abolition of interest rate ceilings for all banks and removing of regulations limiting lending to certain categories of borrowers (for savings institutions).

Second is the growth of wholesale financial markets (generally short-term borrowing from other banks, money market funds, corporate treasurers, and other investors) offering an alternative to retail deposits for banks' funding needs. Most banks that failed in this crisis had large wholesale funding needs. The third is the development of securitization, so banks no longer need to hold loans on balance sheet but can instead package and sell them to other investors, benefiting nonetheless from the sizeable front-end fees from loan origination. Securitization and wholesale markets stem, in turn, from the development of information technology and globalization of financial markets.

Figure 2: "Modern" Bank
"On balance sheet"

Assets	Liabilities
Liquid assets	Capital
Illiquid loans	Retail deposits
Illiquid securities	Wholesale deposits

"Off balance sheet"

Loans being securitized	Illiquid securities
Illiquid securities in SIV/ conduit	Asset-backed commercial paper with bank backup line of credit

The "modern" bank (Figure 2), such as current large US, UK, and European commercial banks, can be seen as a response to these developments that also seeks to maximize profitability by all possible means. Liquid assets are hence reduced to the lowest possible level given their lower return than other assets. Capital is equally held only at the level required by supervisors. In order to grow the balance sheet faster than is feasible with sticky retail deposits, the bank takes on a considerable volume of wholesale funding ("liability management"), although such funding, typically not being covered by deposit insurance and held by well-informed investors, is much more subject to "runs" than retail deposits. Meanwhile, loan growth can be extended beyond that feasible given capital and deposits by ongoing securitization of loans.

Following the Basel 1 agreement in 1988, capital adequacy is counted on a risk-weighted basis. This gives an incentive to hold a proportion of highly rated securities on the asset side if they are also high yielding. The products of securitization, which we call ABS (residential mortgage-backed securities and especially higher-rated tranches of collateralized debt obligations) could provide AAA ratings and high yields and hence proved attractive to banks. However, their opaque nature made them relatively illiquid compared with other types of securities, and the ratings turned out, in retrospect, to be excessively optimistic. The modern bank might also run special investment vehicles or conduits, forms of subsidiary designed to hold similar long-term securities financed by short-term asset-backed commercial paper, where the bank profits from the difference in yield between them. The subsidiaries are supposed to be independent of the bank and their failure should not generate an obligation. However, the bank might nonetheless have an obligation to the subsidiary if it got into difficulty, due to reputation reasons or due to backup lines of credit, as indeed took place in 2007–9.

Regulation of the modern bank is clearly more complex, although the same principles apply. A key issue is liquidity regulation, which needs to consider the risks of wholesale funding as well as low liquid asset holdings. But equally, capital adequacy needed to take account of the more complex risks implicit in the new structure that banks adopted. With securities held as assets, losses can arise from falls in price in the market as well as defaults by borrowers.

The new Basel III proposals for banking regulation include provisions to tighter capital requirements, detailed rules on liquidity, tighter regulation of subsidiaries and of trading, and large systemic institutions to be subject to tighter regulation to try to offset the "too big to fail" problem.[4] There remain questions whether the rules are sufficiently strict, as well as the fact that the new rules do not focus on issues of values and virtues stressed in chapter 3.

---

4. Basel Committee (2011).

Bibliography

Ancient Hebrew Research Center (2006). "Question of the Month—Subdue?" *Biblical Hebrew E-Magazine* 27 (May, 2006). No pages. Online: http://www.ancient-hebrew.org/emagazine/027.rtf.

Bank of England (2008). *Financial Stability Report Issue 24, October 2008*. London: Bank of England.

Barrell, R., and M. Weale (2009). "Fiscal Policy, Fairness between Generations and National Saving." *Oxford Review of Economic Policy* 26: 87–116.

Barrell, R., and E. P. Davis (2008). "The Evolution of the Financial Market Crisis in 2008." *National Institute Economic Review* 206: 5–14.

Barth, K. (1960). *Church Dogmatics III/2. The Doctrine of Creation*. Edited and translated by G. W. Bromiley and T. F. Torrance. Edinburgh: T. & T. Clark.

Basel Committee (2011). "Basel III: A Global Regulatory Framework for More Resilient Banks and Banking Systems—Revised Version June 2011." Basel: Bank for International Settlements.

Beaudoin, T. (2003). *Consuming Faith*. Lanham, MD: Sheed and Ward.

Bieler, A. (2005). *Calvin's Economic and Social Thought*. Geneva: World Alliance of Reformed Churches/World Council of Churches.

Booth, P., editor. (2010). *Christian Perspectives on the Financial Crash*. London: St Paul's.

Bornstein, D. (2005). *The Price of a Dream: The Story of the Grameen Bank*. Oxford: Oxford University Press.

Britton, A., and P. Sedgwick (2003). *Economic Theory and Christian Belief*. Religions and Discourse 16. Oxford: Oxford University Press.

Brueggemann, W. (1977). *The Land: Place as Gift, Promise, and Challenge in Biblical Faith*. Overtures to Biblical Theology. Philadelphia: Fortress.

Clough, D., R. Higginson, and M. Parsons (2009). "Usury, Investment and the Sub-Prime Sector." Research commissioned by UK Church Investors Group. Online: http://www.churchinvestorsgroup.org.uk/system/files/documents/editor/Usury%20%20Investment%20Report%20Final%20June%2008.pdf.

Collier, J. (1992). "Contemporary Culture and the Role of Economics." In *The Gospel and Contemporary Culture*, edited by H. Montefiore, 103–28. London: Mowbray.

Davis, E. P. (1995). *Debt, Financial Fragility and Systemic Risk*. Oxford: Oxford University Press.

———. (2007). "A Confrontation of Economic and Theological Approaches to 'Ending Poverty' in Africa." Brunel University Working Paper 07-14. Online: http://bura.brunel.ac.uk/handle/2438/3523.

———. (2008). "Liquidity, Financial Crises and the Lender of Last Resort—How Much of a Departure Is the Sub-Prime Crisis?" In *Lessons from the Financial Turmoil of 2007 and 2008*, edited by P. Bloxham and C. Kent, 111–35. Sydney: Reserve Bank of Australia.

———. (2009). "Banking on Prudence." In *OECD Report on UK Economy and OECD Economics Department Working Papers 717*. Paris: Organization for Economic Co-operation and Development.

Davis, E. P., and D. Karim (2008). "Could Early Warning Systems Have Helped to Predict the Sub-Prime Crisis?" *National Institute Economic Review* 206: 35–47.

———. (2009). "Macroprudential Regulation—The Missing Policy Pillar." *National Institute Economic Review* 211: 67–80.

Davis, E. P. and B. Steil. (2001). *Institutional Investors*. Cambridge: MIT.

Diamond, D., and P. Dybvig (1983). "Bank Runs, Deposit Insurance, and Liquidity." *Journal of Political Economy* 91: 401–419.

Dickinson, R., and J. Langley. (2009). "Kingdom Economics." *Christianity Magazine*, January 2009: 20–26.

FDIC (2011). "Foreclosure Statistics from NeighborWorks America." Federal Deposit Insurance Corporation. Online http://www.fdic.gov/about/comein/files/fore-closure_statistics.pdf.

Featherby, J. (2009). *The White Swan Formula: Rebuilding Business and Finance for the Common Good*. London: London Institute for Contemporary Christianity. Online: http://www.licc.org.uk/uploaded_media/1245940715-White%20Swan%20Formula%20Web.pdf.

Ferguson, N. (2008). "The Age of Obligation." No pages. Online: http://blogs.ft.com/economistsforum/2008/12/the-age-of-obligation/.

———. (2009). *The Ascent of Money: A Financial Story of the World*. New York: Penguin.

Fitzgerald, V. (1999). "The Economics of Liberation Theology." In *The Cambridge Companion to Liberation Theology*, edited by Christopher Rowland, 218–34. Cambridge: Cambridge University Press.

FSA (2009). *The Turner Review: A Regulatory Response to the Global Financial Crisis*. London: Financial Services Authority.

Goldingay, J. (2006). *Old Testament Theology*. Vol. 2, *Israel's Faith*. Downers Grove, IL: InterVarsity.

Goodchild, P. (2007). *The Theology of Money*. London: SCM.

Graafland, J. J. (2009). "Calvin's Restrictions on Interest: Guidelines for the Credit Crisis." *European Banking Center Discussion Paper No. 2009–22*, University of Tilburg. Online: http://papers.ssrn.com/sol3/papers.cfm?abstract_id=1513173.

Green, S. (1988). *Serving God? Serving Mammon?* London: Marshall Pickering.

———. (2009). *Good Value: Reflections on Money, Morality and an Uncertain World*. London: Allen Lane.

Greene, M. (2010). *The Great Divide*. London: London Institute for Contemporary Christianity.

Gregg, S. (2010). "Credit, Sin and the 2008 Financial Crisis." In *Christian Perspectives on the Financial Crash*, edited by P. Booth, 45–57. London: St Paul's.

Griffin, K., and J. Gurley (1985). "Radical Analyses of Imperialism, the Third World, and the Transition to Socialism: A Survey Article." *Journal of Economic Literature* 23: 1089–1143.

Griffiths, B. (1980). *Morality and the Market Place*. London: Hodder and Stoughton.

———. (1984). *The Creation of Wealth: A Christian Case for Capitalism*. London: Hodder and Stoughton.

———. (2001). "The Culture of the Market." In *Christianity and the Culture of Economics*, edited by D. Hay, 12–32. Cardiff: University of Wales Press.

Harris, R. (2010). "Recourse and Non-Recourse Mortgages: Foreclosure, Bankruptcy, Policy." Tel Aviv: Tel Aviv University Law School. Online: http://ssrn.com/abstract=1591524.

Hay, D. A. (1989). *Economics Today: A Christian Critique.* Leicester: Apollos.

Hendry, D. F. (1984). "Econometric Modelling of House Prices in the UK." In *Econometrics and Quantitative Economics,* edited by D. F. Hendry and K. F. Wallis, 237–60. Oxford: Blackwell.

Hernández-Murillo, R., and D. Roisman (2005). "The Economics of Charitable Giving—What Gives?" *The Regional Economist,* October 2005, 12–13.

Higginson, R. (1993). *Called to Account: Adding Value in God's World.* Guildford, UK: Eagle.

Hoare, R. (2006). "The Theology of Risk-taking." Paper presented at the Forum of Churches Together in the Merseyside Region, Friends Meeting House, Paradise Street, Liverpool, 1 April 2006.

Hobsbawm, E. (1994). *The Age of Extremes: The Short Twentieth Century, 1914–1991.* London: Joseph.

IMF. (2008). *Global Financial Stability Report, October 2008.* Washington, DC: International Monetary Fund.

Merton, R. C., and Z. Bodie. (1995). "A Conceptual Framework for Analyzing the Financial Environment." In *The Global Financial System: A Functional Perspective,* edited by D. Crane et al., 3–31. Cambridge: Harvard Business School Press.

Mills, P. (1993). "The Ban on Interest—Dead Letter or Radical Solution?" *Cambridge Papers.* Cambridge: The Jubilee Centre. No pages. Online: http://www.jubilee-centre.org/document.php?id=3.

———. (2009). "The Economic Crisis: A Biblical Diagnosis and Foundation for Recovery." Paper presented at the Cambridge Papers Open Day, Jubilee Trust, 4 May 2009. No pages. Online: http://www.jubilee-centre.org/uploaded/files/resource_315.pdf.

———. (2011). "The Great Financial Crisis: A Biblical Diagnosis." *Cambridge Papers* 20.1. Cambridge: The Jubilee Centre. No pages. Online: http://www.jubilee-centre.org/document.php?id=414.

Morisy, A. (2011). *Borrowing from the Future: A Faith-Based Approach to Intergenerational Equity.* New York: Continuum.

Muellbauer, J., and A. Murphy. (1997). "Booms and Busts in the UK Housing Market." *Economic Journal* 107: 1701–27.

Nelson, R. H. (1991). *Reaching for Heaven on Earth.* Lanham, MD: Rowman and Littlefield.

Nichols, V. (2008). "Homily Preached at the Civic Mass of the Feast of Christ the King." 23 November 2008, St Chad's Catholic Cathedral, Birmingham. Online: http://catholickey.blogspot.com/2008/11/free-markets-require-virtue.html.

Piper, J. (1986). *Desiring God: Meditations of a Christian Hedonist.* Portland, OR: Multnomah.

Rawls, J. (1971). *A Theory of Justice.* Cambridge: Harvard University Press.

Rayo, L., and G. S. Becker. (2007). "Evolutionary Efficiency and Happiness." *Journal of Political Economy* 115: 307–37.

Reinhart, C. M., and K. S. Rogoff. (2009). *This Time Is Different: Eight Centuries of Financial Folly.* Princeton, NJ: Princeton University Press.

Schluter, M., and R. Clements. (1986). *Reactivating the Extended Family: From Biblical Norms to Public Policy in Britain.* Cambridge: Jubilee Centre Publications. Online: http://www.jubilee-centre.org/uploaded/files/Reactivating%20the%20Extended%20Family.pdf.

SDC. (2009). "Prosperity without Growth?—The Transition to a Sustainable Economy." Sustainable Development Commission Papers (30 March 2009). Online:

http://www.sd-commission.org.uk/data/files/publications/prosperity_without _growth_report.pdf.

Selby, P. (1997). *Grace and Mortgage: The Language of Faith and the Debt of the World*. London: Darton, Longman and Todd.

Sider, R. (1997). *Rich Christians in an Age of Hunger*. 2nd ed. London: Hodder and Stoughton.

Smith, A. (1977). *An Inquiry into the Nature and Causes of the Wealth of Nations*. Chicago: University of Chicago Press.

Smith, K. R. (2005). *God's Economic Mandate? A Perspective on Stewardship Economics*. Eastbourne, UK: Thankful Books.

Treasury Committee. (2008). "The Run on the Rock." *House of Commons Treasury Select Committee Report*. London: UK Parliament. Online: http://www.publications .parliament.uk/pa/cm200708/cmselect/cmtreasy/56/56i.pdf.

Weber, M. (2002). *The Protestant Ethic and the Spirit of Capitalism*. Translated and with an introduction by S. Kalberg. Los Angeles: Roxbury.

Wesley, J. (1996). "The Danger of Riches, Sermon 87." In *Sermons on Several Occasions*. The Christian Classics Ethereal Library. Online: http://www.ccel.org/ccel/wesley/ sermons.vi.xxxiv.html.

White, S., and R. Tiongco. (1997). *Doing Theology and Development: Meeting the Challenge of Poverty*. Edinburgh: St Andrew.

Williams, R. (2008). "Archbishop's Article on the Financial Crisis." *The Spectator* 27, September 2008. No pages. Online: http://www.archbishopofcanterbury.org/ articles.php/629/archbishops-article-on-the-financial-crisis.

Scripture Index

Author Index

Subject Index

Introducing the Author

E. Philip Davis

An economist and minister, Philip Davis is Pastor of Penge Baptist Church, South East London, Senior Research Fellow at the UK National Institute of Economic and Social Research and Associate Professor of Economics and Finance at Brunel University, West London. Before becoming a minister, he spent twenty years working at the Bank of England as an economist and then ten years as a tenured Professor of Economics and Finance at Brunel University, West London, where he was latterly Head of Department. He studied theology at the London School of Theology, graduating in 2007 with a first class degree, and also has an MA and MPhil in Economics from Oxford University.

In economics, his main research interests are financial crises and pension funds, while in theology he has written on poverty and the interface between economics and theology. Earlier books include *Pension Funds, Retirement Income Security and Capital Markets* (Oxford University Press), *Debt, Financial Fragility and Systemic Risk* (Oxford University Press) and *Institutional Investors* (MIT Press). Married with three children, Philip lives with his wife, Claire, in Penge, South East London.

rational
responsible
Relational

ACTORS
FAMILIES
INDIVIDUALS
CHURCHES
SCHOOLS
Vol. Assoc.'s
Gov't's @ many levels